AMERICAN
INDIAN LIVES

POLITICAL
LEADERS
AND
PEACEMAKERS

◆ ◆ ◆

Victoria Sherrow

Facts On File®

AN INFOBASE HOLDINGS COMPANY

For my parents, Charles and Lillian, with love.

On the cover: (left) Spotted Tail; (right) Wilma Mankiller

Political Leaders and Peacemakers

Copyright © 1994 by Victoria Sherrow

Facts On File, Inc.
460 Park Avenue South
New York, NY 10016

Library of Congress Cataloging-in-Publication Data

Sherrow, Victoria.
    Political leaders and peacemakers / Victoria Sherrow.
        p.   cm. — (American Indian lives)
    Includes bibliographical references and index.
    ISBN 0-8160-2943-1 (acid-free paper)
    1. Indians of North America—Biography—Juvenile literature.
    2. Indians of North America—Kings and rulers—Juvenile literature.
    3. Indians of North America—Politics and government—Juvenile
    literature. [1. Indians of North America—Biography.   2. Indians
    of North America—Kings and rulers.   3. Indians of North America—
    Politics and government.]   I. Title.   II. Series: American Indian
    lives (New York, N.Y.)
    E89.S45   1994
    970.004'97'0092—dc20
    [B]   93-38383

A British CIP catalogue record for this book is available from the British Library.

Facts On File books are available at special discounts when purchased in bulk quantities for businesses, associations, institutions, or sales promotions. Please call our Special Sales Department in New York at 212/683-2244 or 800/322- 8755.

Text design by Ellen Levine
Cover design by Nora Wertz
Printed in the United States of America

MP FOF 10 9 8 7 6 5 4 3 2 1

This book is printed on acid-free paper.

CONTENTS

◆ ◆ ◆

ACKNOWLEDGMENTS

◆ ◆ ◆

With special thanks to:

Cheryl Beyal, Navajo Historic Preservation Department
Lydia Bickford, personal assistant to Ada Deer
Nicole Bowen, my editor
Alan Downer, Navajo Historic Preservation Department
John Kahionhes Fadden (Mohawk), Six Nations Indian Museum
Lynn Howard, Cherokee Nation Communications
Stephanie Schultes, Iroquois Indian Museum

INTRODUCTION

◆ ◆ ◆

During the 1500s, a Native American living in present-day New York State had a vision of fellowship among all peoples. He helped to create a type of representative government that united five (later six) tribal nations into the Iroquois League. Known among his people as the Peacemaker, this man foresaw a world in which people followed common principles and laws, guided by leaders they had chosen themselves.

The Peacemaker hoped that these ideals would spread beyond the Iroquois to embrace other peoples. He expressed this hope in these words, as handed down through the centuries:

> A council fire for all nations shall be kindled. It shall be lighted for the Cherokees and for the Wyandots. We will kindle it also for the seven nations living toward the sunrising, and these nations shall light such fires for the peoples living still further toward the sunrising. And we will kindle the fire also for the nations that dwell toward the sunsetting. All shall receive the Great Law and labor together for the welfare of man.

During the time the Peacemaker and his comrade, Hayenwatha, were spreading their message of goodwill and developing the Iroquois confederation, there were hundreds of Native American tribes in North America. For thousands of years, these groups had followed their varying customs and diverse ways of life, which included different styles of government and leadership. Many tribes operated under a system in which the members discussed important issues among themselves and had a voice in choosing their leaders and making decisions.

Indian leaders, called chiefs, exercised power in different ways, depending on the tribe and the situation at hand. Most chiefs were men, but a few tribes had women leaders—something that is more common today. Typically, a group had one or more war chiefs as well as peace chiefs. While war leaders were charged with protecting the group from enemies or planning attacks on outsiders, peace leaders settled disputes within the tribe and guided the people in making decisions about everyday life. Some tribes had separate chiefs for war and peace, while in others, conditions might propel peace-loving chiefs into the role of leading their people through a war.

Tribes also differed in terms of how rigidly they were organized. Some tribes gave their chiefs more authority than others, and individual chiefs might try to assume greater power. But most leaders were obliged to confer with tribal councils, often made up of respected elders of the tribe. Spiritual leaders, who performed ceremonies and rituals, were highly valued and were often consulted, too.

Peace chiefs played a major role in diplomacy. For that reason, tribes tended to choose leaders who were talented orators—often, leaders could speak several Indian dialects, and sometimes English, French, or Spanish as well. In many cases, though, a chief inherited his role. No matter how they gained their positions, chiefs had to show wisdom and ability through their actions. If they did not, their people might ignore their directions or remove and replace them.

The challenges facing Native American leaders became more complex after the 1500s, as white Europeans came onto their lands. At first, many Indians welcomed the newcomers, who came alone or in small groups to fish, trap beaver, or establish small settlements. Some newcomers brought items to trade—metal tools, new kinds of seeds and foods, woven cloth, and blankets, for example. And the continent was large and abundant in resources; there seemed to be plenty of room for all.

Over the years, thousands more Europeans came. They settled up and down the Eastern Seaboard and streamed into the Ohio country, then across the Mississippi River and onto the western

Plains, all the way to the West Coast. By the late 1800s, whites could
be found in every region.

Many whites were ignorant of and disrespectful toward the
knowledge and ways of the Native American peoples. They
viewed North America as a "new world," rather than a land
already settled by millions of people. The natural resources were
seen as being there for the taking. Indians were viewed as a threat
or, at best, an inconvenience. Some colonists, such as those in the
Southwest, even used Indians as slave laborers. Disdainful of
Native religions, these newcomers set out to convert Indians to
their own Christian religions. They had guns and other weapons
the Indians had not seen or used before, and they brought a
catastrophic wave of diseases—smallpox, cholera, influenza, tuberculosis, and measles—to which the Indians had had no previous exposure. As these and other diseases became epidemic,
millions of people died.

A clash between the attitudes and values of the two groups
deepened the problems. The Indians' view of the world directed
them to live in harmony with nature, while whites sought to
change or subjugate nature to fit their goals. Native Americans
found the concepts of ownership and materialism strange, while
whites believed they could buy and sell land and accumulate
goods and resources for themselves.

It is hard to overstate the difficulties Native American leaders
faced during these years of dramatic change. Repeatedly, they had
to make decisions with little information or with incomplete understanding of the whites' language, culture, and intentions. Their
choices shrank as they were engulfed by territorial whites backed
by numerous, well-armed troops. Should they go to war or should
they work for peace? Would cooperation or resistance toward
whites best enable them to survive?

Faced with the loss of their ancestral lands and ways of life, even
with extinction, some fought or fled from their regions, while
others tried to negotiate and find ways to coexist. In their treaty
negotiations, they were often misled and disappointed.

Furthermore, the U.S. government did not have a consistent
way of dealing with Native Americans. Policies might change

from one year to the next. Before the American Revolution, different European nations, including England, France, and Spain, controlled the land and made treaties with the Indians. After the Revolution, the new U.S. government often disregarded these agreements. Many treaties the Indian leaders had made in good faith were voided as U.S. leaders renegotiated and sought new lands, pushing ever farther west.

By the 1830s, the U.S. government wanted eastern tribes to move west of the Mississippi to Indian territory in what is now Oklahoma. The East was now seen as too small to house both whites and Indians who still lived on their ancestral lands. The Cherokee were among the casualties of this removal policy, as it was called. Chief John Ross had to lead his people from the fertile, grassy lands they had occupied for centuries to dry, hot, unfamiliar lands out west. Other tribes were likewise forced to move.

Ross and other leaders, such as Black Kettle of the Cheyenne, Washakie of the Shoshone, and Ouray of the Ute, were thwarted regularly as their lands were narrowed, then finally taken, forcing them to move to other locations. Despite years of friendship with white officials, Washakie spent more than 10 years getting a commitment from the government about where his people could settle. Several more years passed before the lands were safe for the Shoshone to occupy.

In order to divide and conquer, whites also sometimes pitted different tribes against one another, further challenging the leaders. Distributing land at will, the government sometimes ignored an agreement it had made with one tribe, granting the same land to a different tribe. At times, former enemies were sent to live together on the same reservation. This happened to arguing factions of the Cherokee in the early 1800s and to the Shoshone and Arapaho in the late 1800s.

As U.S. officials proposed various new treaties, Indian leaders debated whether they should sign, and exactly what they were signing. Could they trust the U.S. officials to keep their promises? They were offered benefits if they did sign and threatened if they refused. Frequently, as Crowfoot of the Blackfoot and other chiefs discovered, the promised benefits were not forthcoming.

When white officials could not get legitimate Indian leaders to agree with them, they sometimes signed agreements with more cooperative leaders whom Indians called "government chiefs." These chiefs might represent only a small band of a particular tribe, but government officials would claim they had authority to negotiate for the entire tribe.

During the late 1800s, tribal leaders faced more changes and disruptions. They had signed treaties that gave them specific reservations on which to live and financial aid or material goods as compensation for their losses. In many cases, they received less land, goods, and money than they had been promised. Then U.S. policy shifted again, as Congress passed the General Allotment Act of 1887, also known as the Dawes Act. The act aimed to turn Indians into farmers by placing them on small, individual plots of land. Larger reservations were divided, often despite a tribe's strong objections.

What land remained was offered for sale to whites. More than 90 million acres of Indian lands were sold at that time, often at absurdly low prices or through coercion. Ancestral lands, already sharply reduced, shrank once again by millions of acres.

In the 20th century, the government developed a new policy called termination. The goal was that Indians be assimilated into the general population, eventually leaving the reservations. States were given more control over reservations within their borders. As Ada Deer wrote in her autobiography, "The policy called for an end to federal aid and protection, an end to the reservation system, and, of course, would mean a substantial savings to the Congressional pocketbook." Deer knew the negative effects of termination quite well: In 1954 her tribe, the Menominee of Wisconsin, were the first to be "terminated." Deer and other Menominee worked to restore the group's tribal status, and the termination was eventually reversed by the U.S. Supreme Court.

By 1961, government leaders, under the administration of President John F. Kennedy, called the termination program a failure. More people became aware of the problems Indians had faced through the years and began to understand that Indians have a right to their own ways, customs, and religions. Government leaders recognized that tribes needed an economic base and a certain amount of land. They should not be forced to conform, change religions, or be assimilated except by choice.

From 1963 to 1968, President Lyndon B. Johnson proposed new education and health care funding as part of his antipoverty programs. His successor, Richard M. Nixon, asked Congress to restore some ancestral Indian lands, such as the Blue Lake region of the Taos Pueblo, and to pass a religious freedom bill.

The Indian leaders who emerged during these years were articulate and well-educated, often using the educational, legal, and political systems to voice their concerns. Some entered mainstream American politics, besides holding official positions within their tribes. Leaders worked to raise Native American pride and renew ideals, as well as to increase public awareness of Indian history and the mistreatment Indians had endured through the years. The American Indian Movement (AIM) of the 1960s and 1970s, led by energetic leaders such as Chippewas Clyde Bellecourt and Dennis Banks, sometimes used more militant methods—even force—to bring public attention to their cause. Groups such as the Shoshone, spurred by sisters Mary and Carrie Dann, and the Iroquois, led by Leonard Rickard, fought for treaty rights in the courts.

Woman assumed more visible roles. Annie Wauneka of the Navajo was among those who brought attention to Native American health problems. In 1987 Wilma Mankiller, a Cherokee, became the first woman elected to lead a tribe. Today about 8 percent of tribal chiefs are women.

Centuries of experience in problem-solving and diplomacy echo in the words of these leaders as they cope with contemporary issues—health care, education, unemployment, poverty. Today's leaders are more likely to be seen in dresses or suits than in Native Indian dress. They have lived on reservations as well as off, and they include writers, educators, social workers, scientists, and other professionals. They understand contemporary society and have a vision of how people can adapt and grow. Yet they may also be traditional leaders, attending religious ceremonies such as a tribal powwow or Sun Dance. As Wilma Mankiller says, "In my

A monument to Chief Seathl in Pioneer Square, Seattle, by artist Hachivi Heap-of-Birds. The left panel reads, "Now the streets are our home" while the right one translates to "Faraway brothers and sisters, we still remember you." (Photo by Kris Murphy)

generation . . . we're trying to figure out a balance between the two worlds. . . . I try to incorporate as many of the old values as I can."

The Native Americans in this volume have been chosen to show major developments in Indian life during different periods in history. Their life stories show the problems faced by Native Americans as a whole and the specific dilemmas of several individual tribes. These people represent various Indian cultural groups—Eastern Woodlands, Southern, Plains, Southwestern, Western, and Pacific Coastal—and include both men and women.

Through the centuries, as Native American leaders have sought peace and justice and have worked to help their tribes survive, they have often spoken eloquently about their problems and dreams. Some of their words have been recorded and quoted through the years. In 1854, speaking of his people's plight with

resignation and foresight, Chief Seathl of the Suquamish had this
to say:*

> We know that the white man does not understand our ways. One
> portion of the land is the same to him as the rest, for he is a stranger
> who comes in the night and takes from the land whatever he needs.
> The earth is not his brother . . . and when he has conquered it, he
> moves on. He leaves his fathers' graves and his children's birthright
> is forgotten.
>
> The noble braves, fond mothers, glad happy-hearted maidens,
> and even the little children, who lived and rejoiced here for a brief
> season, and whose very names are now forgotten, still love these
> sombre solitudes and their deep fastnesses which, at eventide,
> grow shadowy with the presence of dusky spirits. . . . The white
> man will never be alone. Let him be just and deal kindly with my
> people, for the dead are not powerless. Dead—did I say? There is
> no death. Only a change of worlds.

---

*For the sake of accuracy, quotations by Chief Seathl have been taken from accounts of his
speeches recorded during his life.

DEGANAWIDAH AND HAYENWATHA

◆ ◆ ◆

Architects of The Great Peace

Long before white European settlers formed colonies in North America, there was already a united nation there—the *Hodenosaunee*, or League of the Iroquois. Around 1450, five (later six) groups of Native Americans living in an area that now includes upper New York State and parts of eastern Canada agreed to live in peace under a common set of laws. This remarkable agreement produced the Confederacy of Five Nations and a democratic style of government that influenced 18th-century U.S. leaders, including Benjamin Franklin and the men who wrote the Constitution.

These Native Americans had a system that gave them individual liberty and a voice in who would lead them, and how. In his 1727 history of the Iroquois, Cadwallader Colden wrote,

> Each Nation is an absolute Republick by its self, govern'd in all Publick Affairs of War and Peace by the Sachems or Old Men whose Authority and Power is gain'd by and consists wholly in the Opinion the rest of the Nation have of their Wisdom and Integrity. They never execute their Resolutions by Compulsion or Force upon any of their people. Honour and Esteem are their Principal Rewards, as Shame & being Despised are their Punishments.

In rich detail, history mingles with legend in the Iroquois account of how the Confederacy was born through the efforts of two idealistic leaders: Deganawidah (also spelled Deganawida or Dekaniwidah), called the Peacemaker or Heavenly Messenger, and Hayenwatha (also spelled Ainwatha or Hiawatha). During the 1800s, the Iroquois told the story of the Confederacy, as it had been passed from generation to generation, to interested white Americans, who then wrote down their accounts.

The whites did not fully understand some of the unfamiliar symbols or religious ideas. Some mistakenly thought that Hayenwatha was a god figure, not a real person. A 19th-century writer, Henry R. Schoolcraft, mixed up the facts and wrote a series of tales in which Hayenwatha is a Chippewa god. New England author Henry Wadsworth Longfellow repeated the error when he made Hayenwatha a Chippewa hero in his famous 1855 epic poem, *Hiawatha*.

In the late 1800s, J. N. B. Hewitt, a Tuscarora and a respected scientist at the Smithsonian Institution's Bureau of American Ethnology, worked to sort out the story. He recorded Iroquois versions of the history of the Confederacy and wrote a series of publications that describe Hayenwatha as a real person. Hewitt's writings are thought to be a fairly accurate written account of Hayenwatha and the Peacemaker. Dr. William N. Fenton, an expert on Iroquois history, added new insights during the 1900s that upheld Hewitt's main conclusions.

These two 15th-century leaders, Deganawidah and Hayenwatha, achieved a remarkable feat when they unified the five tribes. The Oneida, Onondaga, Cayuga, Seneca, and Mohawk had long been bitter rivals. By the 1400s, these woodland groups had endured years of sorrow, fighting over territory and over hunting and fishing rights. They spent much time and effort preparing for war. The tribes followed the custom of blood revenge, which required warriors to kill a member of a group who had killed one of theirs. The people had a saying that the sun must love war, because peace was so rare at that time. As translated by J. N. B. Hewitt, the Iroquois history related that "everywhere there was misery."

Yet their religious heritage taught these peoples that the Master of Life, who had created the world, wished people to live in peace and love. His evil brother had led people astray, said the creation story, and so the Master, Teharonhiawagon, promised that someday he would send an ambassador to help restore the good. As the killing and sorrow went on, people waited and hoped.

◆ ◆ ◆

Deganawidah (henceforth called the Peacemaker, in accord with Iroquois custom) was born into the Wendot tribe—whom the French later called the Huron—near what is now Kingston, Ontario in Canada. His exact birthdate is unknown but may have been in the early-to-mid 1400s. According to legend, his mother was poor and lived with her mother, both lacking a clan membership. She had a dream in which she was told to give her son his name (which may have meant "double row of teeth") but that he would one day cause the ruin of his tribe. For that reason, the Peacemaker's grandmother tried to drown the infant, plunging him three times into icy water. Each time, he survived, appearing back beside them in the morning.

The Peacemaker was known for his honesty and good looks, but he grew up lonely. Others teased him because he stammered and rejected war toys and games. Like his mother, the Peacemaker had visions. In one dream, he saw a huge white pine tree that stretched skyward, its limbs reaching into the land of the Master of Life. The Peacemaker believed that the tree represented a unified society, with the four white roots stretched in four directions to carry the message of peace.

The pine tree got strength from its soil, which the Peacemaker said was nourished by three sets of double principles of life. The double principle was health of the body and of the mind. The three principles were peace between individuals and groups; righteousness in conduct, thought, and speech, leading to equity and justice among peoples; and physical strength and civil authority—known as the power of the Orenda.

After his own group rejected his ideas, the Peacemaker set out to find people who would follow his teachings. Because of his

This drawing by Mohawk artist John Fadden shows the Peacemaker planting the Tree of Peace. (Courtesy of John Fadden)

speech impediment, people were not inclined to listen carefully to his words. One version of the story says that the Peacemaker crossed Lake Ontario to what is now upstate New York, where he found a woman who fed him and accepted his message of peace and friendship—The Great Peace, as it would soon be called. The Peacemaker named her Jigonsasee (New Face) and said that hereafter, she would be the Great Peace Woman.

At some point, the Peacemaker met Hayenwatha (whose name comes from *Haio-hwa'tha*: "he keeps them awake" or perhaps "he who combs" in Mohawk). Born an Onondaga sometime in the early 1400s, Hayenwatha was later adopted by the turtle clan of the Mohawk Nation after he began his peacemaking work. Little is known of his early life, but he may have married the daughter of a chief and become a medicine man or chief himself, with a family of several daughters. An influential man and a fine orator, Hayenwatha promoted new ideas of reform. He invited members of the surrounding villages to attend a peace council, but a fierce Onondaga chief named Tadodaho (also spelled Atatorho) came and prevented the participants from reaching an agreement.

A painting by Mohawk artist John Fadden shows Hayenwatha grieving over the death of his children, holding a string of shell beads, called wampum, in his right hand. (Schoharie Museum of the Iroquois Indian, #M158)

Tadodaho ruled like a tyrant, using spies to gather information about his opponents, and killing those who defied him. He is pictured as crooked in body, with hands standing out from his body like those of a turtle, and with claws instead of toes on his feet. His hair is likened to a twisted mass of snakes.

Each time a meeting was planned to reform and lead to peace, Tadodaho upset it one way or another, thwarting the peace-minded rulers. When Hayenwatha's eldest daughter sickened and died shortly after the first meeting, people feared that Tadodaho's evil magic had caused her death. Yet Hayenwatha bravely called another meeting. Again, Tadodaho and his warriors showed up to intimidate the participants, and once more, Hayenwatha lost a daughter to illness and death. It seemed there could be no peace.

A poignant story describes the death of Hayenwatha's last daughter. Grieving, he tried one final time to meet with the Onondaga. His daughter, who was pregnant, was in the woods gathering firewood when Tadodaho suddenly stood up and cried, "Look at the sky!" An eagle was falling through the air into the woods. As people rushed to vie for its coveted feathers, they trampled the young woman and her unborn child to death.

In anguish, an embittered Hayenwatha left his people to wander in the forest, living in lodges made of hemlock boughs. In one version of the story, he became so grief-stricken that his mind also became crooked. There are different explanations for how the Peacemaker met Hayenwatha. A common one is that the Peacemaker found Hayenwatha mourning in the wilderness, wearing white shells around his neck as a sign of peace. The Peacemaker comforted Hayenwatha, using words that are still repeated in Iroquois condolence ceremonies. The Peacemaker declared that Hayenwatha's eyes, ears, and voice were clogged with grief, but that they should now be opened and made straight.

Discovering that they shared a common goal of peace, the two men set out to convert the five tribes. Hayenwatha had the oratorical skills to convince people to give some thought to their ideas about how their organized groups could work together. The Peacemaker was a neutral or tribeless person, so his messages were more acceptable to other nations.

The two men envisioned a league like an extended family, with local kinship groups (clans) that governed themselves and leaders who would govern the village and the whole tribe. The ideals of brotherhood and equality they now proposed contrasted sharply with the ferocious warlike behavior the Iroquois had shown in the past during battle or while torturing prisoners. They set out to unite these people. The five tribes in the north lived in some 200 villages stretching from the St. Lawrence River to Ohio and Pennsylvania.*

The Iroquois villages consisted of rectangular buildings called longhouses, built along streams or lakes and usually surrounded by log walls for protection. The fertile soil allowed the Indians to grow beans, corn, and squash, so villages were permanent rather than temporary or seasonal.

The two leaders went by canoe from village to village, asking the Mohawk, Oneida, Onondaga, Seneca, and Cayuga to renounce violence. Old resentments were not easily forgotten, and no tribe wished to look cowardly by giving in first. The Oneida said they would join, but only if the Mohawk agreed. After that, the Seneca joined the group, and the Cayuga agreed but only if the Onondaga first promised peace. The Onondaga, under Chief Tadodaho, continued to resist the notion of unity among the tribes.

Once again, the two leaders paddled toward the Onondaga village to urge peace. One story says that in persuading Tadodaho, they made 13 strings of wampum beads and sang six special songs to straighten out his twisted mind. After he was made right in both body and mind, he accepted their idea. The notion of straightening Tadodaho's snakelike coils of hair may have symbolized the use of diplomacy in persuading him to change his ways. The men agreed that the seat of the confederacy, with its ever-burning fire, would be in the land of the Onondaga. An Onondaga was appointed firekeeper and moderator of the regular meetings of the Council of the Great Peace.

Now that the League of the Great Peace was formed, the five tribes presented a united front to other Indians, as well as to the French explorers who began coming onto their land during the 1500s through the Gulf of St. Lawrence. French explorers were told by the Algonquian and the Huron that these tribes were Iriakoiw (rattlesnakes), which led them to call the group *Iroquois*.

---

*Much later, another Iroquois-speaking group, the Tuscarora from North Carolina and Tennessee, were also asked to join.

The Peacemaker had planted the Tree of Peace and presented the Great Law. At the council fire, during a meeting that took place at least once every five years, the group's leaders recited these words, still used today:

> Into our bundle we have gathered the causes of war, and have cast this bundle away. Yea, we even uprooted a tall pine tree, making a very deep hole in the earth, and at the bottom of this hole runs a swift water current. Into this current have we thrown the causes of wars and strife. Our great-grandchildren shall not see them, for we have set back in its former place the great tall pine tree.

The new government was unlike anything these people had yet experienced or that existed at that time in white cultures. It included tribal chiefs, nominated by clan matrons and elected by the people of their village. The chiefs dealt with internal relations among the member tribes. Women could remove these men from office if they were deemed ineffective, after first giving them three warnings. Local clan leaders met in a larger group to make decisions about their leadership.

The League's constitution said of the chiefs that "their hearts shall be full of peace and good will, and their minds filled with yearning for the welfare of the people." None of the chief leaders could be warriors, since warriors might be inclined to advance warlike notions. A key position in the confederacy was one that honored the Peacemaker—the position of pine tree chief, a nonhereditary chief who had to earn his position through special ability and through courage, wisdom, and honesty. It was thought that a worldly office would offend the founder. The spirits of Hayenwatha and the Peacemaker were thought to be present at all council fires after their deaths.

The government was organized so that the Onondaga had 14 leaders, the Cayuga 10, the Mohawk and Oneida nine each, and the Seneca eight. But all decisions had to be unanimous, so these differences in the number of representatives did not actually affect final decisions. Also, the leaders of each tribe had to discuss and agree upon issues so that they would speak with a united voice at the larger gatherings.

After the League was founded, it was said that the Peacemaker set off in his white stone canoe down Lake Onondaga. Hayenwatha, however, continued their work. He may have convinced some Erie, some Huron and some Neutral to join the League. Some stories say that Hayenwatha also visited the Shawnee, Delaware, Miami, and other groups near Lake Superior, possibly even reaching the Mississippi River. Hayenwatha brought back strings of wampum shells, showing that he had spoken with leaders of various tribes. Afterward, he stayed among his people as a revered chief and advisor, developing a system of trails and waterways that linked isolated Iroquois villages. The revered leader died at an old age.

Chances for peace between the Iroquois and other groups diminished as more whites came to the region. The lucrative fur trade led to more competition and conflict among the tribes, as they competed to trap beavers, whose pelts could be traded to whites in exchange for guns and other goods. As conflicts increased, other Indians asked the League for protection, citing their agreement with the principles of the Peacemaker. Among those who allied themselves with the League were the Leni-Lenape (Delaware), the Piscataway from the Potomac River, the Nanticoke from Maryland, and the Saponi and Tutelo from Virginia.

In 1715 the Tuscarora to the south joined the "longhouse" of the Iroquois as equal partners, becoming the sixth Nation. The League was gaining strength, extending into the territory of the Delaware Indians, and might have gone from the western Great Lakes to the Atlantic had not the white colonists interfered.

An early French historian, Bacqueville de la Potherie, wrote that the Iroquois were fine orators. He also said, "They are the Fiercest and most Formidable People in North America and at the same time as Politick and Judicious as well can be conceiv'd." De la Potherie knew French officials who had met in council meetings with the Six Nations.

A Jesuit priest later said that the Iroquois and Huron were "more inclined to practice virtue than the other nations." He spoke of their capacity for "refined feelings."

In 1754, colonial leader Benjamin Franklin proposed the Albany Plan of Union for the colonies. Showing his awareness of the Iroquois League, he said,

> It would be a strange thing if Six Nations of ignorant savages should be capable of forming a scheme for such an union and be able to execute it in such a manner as that it has subsisted ages and appears indissoluble; and yet that a like union should be impracticable for ten or a dozen English colonies, to whom it is more necessary and must be more advantageous, and who cannot be supposed to want an equal understanding of their interests.

In recent years, historians have noted that James Madison, chief writer of the U.S. Constitution, was also familiar with the Iroquois system. Some scholars say that the president and his cabinet resemble the honorary Pine Tree Chiefs, and point out that the U.S. government uses a central place as the capital, as the Iroquois do with their annual Great Council meeting in Onondaga territory, in a long bark- covered house. Both governments have branches to deal with external affairs. (For the Iroquois, the Council of Chiefs, the hereditary leaders, handle external affairs.)

The Iroquois system influenced political thinkers in other nations, too. They could read about it in *League of the Ho-De-No-Sau-Nee, or Iroquois*, an 1851 book in which Lewis Henry Morgan detailed his study of the Iroquois system. Another book, in 1877, elaborated on the principles of the League and was read by two important German thinkers, Karl Marx and Friedrich Engels.

To this day the Iroquois conduct a Grand Council Fire at the capital near Onondaga, New York, representing the people who live south of Canada and at another gathering near Brantford, Ontario. They tell the story of the Great Peace created through the efforts of the Peacemaker and Hayenwatha. In *The Patriot Chiefs*, author Alvin M. Josephy, Jr., points out that their conceptions of "brotherhood and peace . . . are still earnestly yearned for by the parliaments and United Nations of twentieth century humanity." The notion of casting all weapons of war into a pit and planting above it a flourishing tree of peace is an ideal that humankind still strives for.

SEATHL

◆ ◆ ◆

Diplomat of the Pacific Northwest

Strange and distressing things were happening near present-day
Puget Sound in Washington State in the late 1780s. An unfamiliar
disease had spread among the Indians, leaving many dead and
others with disfiguring scars on their faces and bodies. From their
dugout canoes, they saw large, unfamiliar objects at sea off their
peaceful coast. These objects looked to the Indians like huge sea
animals that had white wings or trees sprouting from their backs.

Later they would come to know that this devastating disease—
smallpox—had been brought to the Pacific Northwest by explorers and fishermen from Europe. The strange seagoing objects were
ships. Yet these things reminded the coastal Indians of ancient
prophecies that foretold the end of the world. When pale-skinned
men wearing odd clothing appeared on their shores, it seemed to
confirm that these prophecies were coming true.

Into this atmosphere was born a man who would guide his
group of Coastal Salish people through years of stress and change.
Later, the city of Seattle would be named in his honor, becoming
the largest American city to be named after a Native American.

◆ ◆ ◆

Seathl is thought to have been born around 1786. His father,
Schweabe, a Suquamish (a name that comes from words meaning
"clear salt water"), was a war leader and tribal chief, or headman.
Seathl's mother, Scholitza, was a Duwamish, and is thought to

have been a slave before her marriage. (Some Indian tribes kept those captured in war as slaves.) Because of this, Seathl had to overcome the stigma that some coastal tribes associated with his "low birth," based on his mother's status. The family lived in Seathl's father's house on Blakely Island, and he was probably born there.

Seathl was a young boy in 1792 when the English explorer George Vancouver sailed his ship *Discovery* into Puget Sound. Vancouver had come to survey and draw maps of the Pacific coast. As the *Discovery* reached the coastline, the Indians happened to be celebrating the time of the butterclams. Each May, they camped on Restoration Point on Bainbridge Island to fish and to harvest clams and wild onions. Legend says that Seathl was on the Point and was awed when he saw the great ship arrive.

Curious, the Indians went to the ship to see the strangers and to trade with them, as did other coastal Indians. Most likely, Seathl had not seen any white men before this time. Unlike natives living on the east coast of North America, these coastal Indians had not had contact with whites during the previous two centuries. They spent much of their time fishing and preserving their catch for winter, with salmon being the mainstay of their diet. Sometimes they conducted raids on enemies such as the Cowichan and Yakima; other times, they defended themselves from raids. Such attacks were more feared after the 1780s as tribes in the lower Columbia region got guns and ammunition through trade with whites.

In his youth, Seathl was a warrior who conducted successful raids on other local tribes. His tribe admired his clever plans of attack and his boldness in battle. It may have been these achievements that enabled him to take the honored name *Seathl*, that of his father's father, around the year 1806.

Seathl was about 20 years old when he became one of the chiefs of his tribe. During various raids, he had amassed *hiqwa*, or shell money, taken from enemy tribes, making him both wealthy and successful. He married, and his first child, known as Princess Angeline, was born around 1811. It is thought that during his lifetime, Seathl had two wives and six children, four of whom died young. As was also the custom for wealthy men, he owned Indian slaves.

Seathl probably took part in raids led by the famous Suquamish headman, Kitsap. In 1825 Kitsap organized a large raid against an enemy tribe, the Cowichan peoples who lived around Victoria Harbor on Vancouver Island. Kitsap's group won a battle that became famous in Suquamish history. It was said that during the fierce fighting, 160 of the group's 200 canoes were lost, with their crews.

By 1830 more whites were moving into the Puget Sound area. When one group of explorers landed that year, the Suquamish were on the beach at Elliot Bay celebrating the summer's first run of good salmon. Seathl greeted the white men, explaining why so many people were on the beach: "As the salmon are our chief food we always rejoice to see them coming early and in abundance." He also told the whites, "We want your blankets, your guns, axes, clothing, and tobacco . . . and so we welcome you to our country to make flour, sugar, and other things that we can trade for."

The Suquamish frequently visited a new trading post run by the Hudson Bay Company, where they traded for cloth, metal tools, and guns. A man named Dr. Tolmie saw Seathl during these days and wrote in his diary that the chief was "a brawny Suquamish with a Roman countenance and black curley hair, the handsomest Indian I have ever seen."

Through the white settlers, the Indians were introduced to customs that seemed strange to them. One of these was the practice of signing their marks to show agreement on various written documents—among the Suquamish and other tribes, a man's word alone had always been regarded as sufficient to establish trust. In 1832 some officials at the trading post began teaching Christianity to the Indians. One Englishman, Francis Herron, hoped to end the custom of blood revenge, in which Indians took the life of someone whose tribe had killed one of their members. Seathl was among the leaders who agreed to end this practice.

French missionaries also came to Puget Sound, bringing new religious ideas and rituals to the local tribes. Like the Indians of the Plains and elsewhere, Pacific coastal Indians had been impressed by the white man's power and weapons. They thought white religious practices might account for this power. The Suquamish amazed the missionaries by quickly learning to sing the hymns correctly, without knowing what the French words meant.

Through his acquaintance with the French, Seathl decided to convert to the Catholic religion, possibly around 1838. He took *Noah* as his Christian name. Seathl maintained ties to his native religion and rituals, but he encouraged certain Catholic traditions and held prayer services with his people twice a day, morning and evening.

The prospect of quick riches lured still more white settlers west during the California Gold Rush of 1849. By then, Seathl's father and the other primary headman, Kitsap, had died. Seathl was now the principal chief of his people, who included Suquamish, Duwamish, and other bands of coastal Salish Indians.

Over the years, Seathl had come to believe that making peace with whites was the most reasonable way to ensure that his tribe would survive. For their part, whites saw the chief as an ally, especially after he was baptized. Some Indians, especially the young men, resented Seathl's religious conversion and vigorously protested the stream of white settlers. The chief had to use diplomacy and his reputation as a strong leader to get along with both groups during these difficult years.

When whites established a permanent settlement called Alki Point in Puget Sound in 1851, they were greeted enthusiastically by about 1,000 Indians, who vied for the chance to set up their own houses near those of the settlers. Seathl encouraged friendship and trade with the newcomers. He urged the whites to set up a trading post in his territory, but instead they built it across the bay on the eastern shore. Because Seathl and the other Indians were peaceful, the white settlement was able to flourish.

Another group of settlers, led by Dr. David Maynard, built a community and store within Seathl's territory. Grateful for the chief's friendship, the settlers changed the name of their settlement to Seattle in 1852. While this gave Seathl more recognition and was considered an honor among the whites, Seathl did not approve.

Indian spiritual beliefs taught that it was bad luck to use a person's name while he or she was alive.

Meanwhile, as more white settlers came to Puget Sound, some members of Seathl's tribe continued to protest and many Indians worried that the whites meant to drive them away. They knew that in other parts of the country, Indians were being deprived of their ancestral lands and moved onto reservations. Despite Seathl's pleas for peace, by 1854, some tribal groups were so angry they wanted to expel the whites by force.

The fears of these Indians heightened when the newly ap-pointed governor of the Pacific Northwest, Isaac Stevens, visited the region that same year. Stevens approached various leaders and made it clear that the government wanted to take or reduce the lands occupied by the Indians, moving them onto reservations.

Hundreds of Seathl's people had gathered to see Stevens's arrival. One onlooker said of the scene, "The bay swarmed with canoes and the shore was lined with a living mass of swaying, writhing, dusky humanity, until old Chief Seattle's trumpet tones rolled over the immense multitude like the reveille of a bass drum, when silence became instantaneous and perfect." Seathl, already known as a great orator, made a famous speech that day, stressing the differences between Indian ways and white ways.

Seathl spoke in the Salish dialect. His words were translated into Chinook jargon—a language that whites and Indians used in trade relations—so that Governor Stevens could understand him. A noted linguist, Dr. Henry A. Smith, for whom Smith Cove, Washington, is named, was asked to translate the speech. He took notes during the speech and wrote an English version that has come to be regarded as a relatively faithful account of what Seattle said that day.

> The son [Stevens] of the White Chief [the U.S. president] says his father sends us greetings of friendship and good will. This is kind of him, for we know he has little need of our friendship in return because his people are many. They are like the grass that covers the vast prairies, while my people are few. They resemble the scattering trees of a storm-swept plain.
>
> There was a time when our people covered the land as the waves of a wind-ruffled sea covered its shell-paved floor, but that time has

long since passed away with the greatness of the tribes that are now but a mournful memory. I will not dwell on, nor mourn over, our untimely decay, nor reproach my paleface brothers with hastening it as we too may have been somewhat to blame. . . . But let us hope that the hostilities between the Red Man and his paleface brother may never return. We would have everything to lose and nothing to gain.

Every part of this country is sacred to my people. Every hillside, every valley, every plain and grove has been hallowed by some fond memory or some sad experience of my tribe. Even the rocks, which seem to lie dumb as they swelter in the sun along the silent sea shore in solemn grandeur, thrill with memories of past events connected with the lives of my people.

Seathl went on to warn the whites about the possibility that their civilization, too, might decay if they did not take care of the land and its creatures. In the course of his speech, Seathl spoke resignedly about the fact that he knew his people would be expected to live on the reservation the whites offered them. He said that his people intended to "dwell in peace."

When Isaac Stevens took office as governor of the Washington Territory in January 1855, one of his first acts was to assemble the tribes of Puget Sound and ask them to sign the Treaty of Fort Elliot. This treaty would take control of their lands out of their hands and require them to live on reservations.

Seathl was the first leader to sign the treaty. At age 69, the chief had proven himself in battle as a young man and, during his years as chief, in diplomacy. His words and actions had shown insight into the changing world his people now faced, although this realization was mixed with resignation and sadness. He knew that his people were vastly outnumbered and that the white government had the power to impose its will. By signing the treaty, Seathl and his people agreed to move to the reservation. They were promised certain goods and payments in return. A separate group of Duwamish did not accept the treaty and refused to go voluntarily to a reservation.

Later, when the Suquamish did not receive all they had been promised, Seathl wrote a letter, now in the National Archives, describing their plight and explaining how badly his people

The only known individual portrait of the great Seathl, Suquamish-Duwamish chief, taken a few years before his death. (Historical Society of Seattle and King County, Museum of History and Industry)

needed the things they had been promised in return for their land. Poverty and disease plagued the Fort Kitsap reservation, yet the agents of the Bureau of Indian Affairs did little, partly because the economy was so poor during the Civil War years.

Resentments festered among the Indians, finally erupting in the Yakima War of 1855–56. Tribes living east of the Cascade Mountains began the conflict. Some Nisqually who lived west of the Cascades attacked the Suquamish settlement in January 1856, but Seathl's people resisted, aided by government troops.

Conflicts continued among Indians and settlers for several years after that, but Seathl managed to keep his people at peace. The Suquamish remained on a reservation, in the western part of Puget Sound near what is now Bremerton, Washington. Seathl lived in a large community building called Old Man House. The 60×900 foot building may have been the site of ceremonies he attended as a child, such as the potlatch, a special community meeting at which people gave out gifts. He attended his last potlatch in 1862.

During his last years, Seathl lived on a small pension from the government and spent time with his children and grandchildren or at tribal councils where his advice was sought. He dressed simply in old pants and a shirt, often wrapping a blanket over his shoulders on cold days. In 1863, upon hearing the words of President Abraham Lincoln's Emancipation Proclamation, he was moved to free his eight Indian slaves.

The elderly chief still impressed people with his stately bearing and his speaking skills. Dr. Smith, who had translated his 1954 speech, later wrote that Seathl was the largest Indian he had ever seen "and by far, the noblest looking. He stood nearly six feet in his moccasins and was broad shouldered, deep-chested and finely proportioned. His eyes were large, intelligent, expressive and friendly when in repose. . . ." Smith also described the chief's speaking style: "deep-toned, sonorous, and eloquent sentences rolled from his lips."

Seathl sometimes visited the photographic gallery of E. M. Sammis, located at what is now Main and First Avenue South in Seattle. Sammis had taken photographs of the Pacific Northwest, and one day, the photographer asked Seathl if he would consent

Visitors can see the gravesite of the chief at Suquamish, a village not far from the busy port city of Seattle. (Photo by Kris Murphy)

to pose for a picture. The resulting photograph is the only known portrait of Chief Seathl.

When Seathl died on June 7, 1866, both Indians and white admirers attended his funeral. His gravesite was in the village of Suquamish, near Seattle, which went on to become a thriving American port city. His people still worried about whether his spirit could be at rest, considering that his name was being used for the city.

White settlers soon greatly outnumbered the group of Indians Seathl had led, but the growth of the region owed a great deal to the chief. He had been the whites' ally at a critical time in history, and he left a legacy through his words that is meaningful for all Americans to this day.

JOHN ROSS

◆ ◆ ◆

Leading a Displaced People

On a summer day in 1843, a slender, serious-looking man of medium height stood before a large group of Native Americans. He was John Ross, the 53-year-old principal chief of the Cherokee. His listeners were members of 17 different tribes who had gath-

John Ross convened the famous council of different tribes in June 1843 in Tahlequah, Oklahoma. This painting by John Mix Stanley is part of the collection of the U.S. National Museum. (©Smithsonian Institution, neg. #1063w)

ered in the town of Tahlequah, the new Cherokee capital. It was located on the reservation in Oklahoma (then called Indian Territory) to which the Cherokee had been sent by force. Ross needed to find the right words to comfort and guide the people during this tragic time in their history.

Problems were not new to John Ross. During his years as chief, he had faced many difficult decisions as he led his people during years of momentous change. Only five years earlier, the Cherokee had been forcibly removed from land their ancestors had occupied for thousands of years. The Yun-wi-yah (principal people), as they called themselves, were the last of the five great southeastern Indian nations* to lose their lands to the U.S. government.

The Cherokee then had been forced to travel across the country without enough food, clothing, or blankets to protect themselves against the wet, bitterly cold weather. Most of them had to go on foot along what became known as the Trail of Tears. Almost a third of the 13,000 Cherokee died along the way. One of the soldiers who supervised this forced migration went on to see many bloody battles during the Civil War. Yet he later said, "The Cherokee Removal was the cruelest work I ever knew."

The hot, dry region in the West known as Indian Territory was far different from the fertile Cherokee homelands, rich in rivers and forests, in what is now Tennessee, Georgia, and North and South Carolina. Here, they had to make many adjustments, and the Cherokee disagreed about how they should handle the problems they faced. As their leader, Ross hoped that this gathering, attended by some 10,000 people, would identify some common goals and develop unity among the different factions of the tribe.

Ross thus began the task of leading these divided, dispirited people who had once been so strong and self-sufficient. Ross served his tribe for more than 40 years, helping to develop a constitution, an organized system of government, a newspaper, and a school system. Familiar to several U.S. presidents, the eloquent and resourceful chief was called the "Indian Prince." Among his own people, Ross was known as Coowescoowe, "the egret."

---

*Besides the Cherokee, the Five Civilized Tribes, as they were known, included the Choctaw, Chickasaw, Creek, and Seminole.

◆ ◆ ◆

John Ross was born on October 3, 1790, in Tahnoovayah, on the Coosa River in Georgia. His ancestry included several Scotsmen. His maternal grandfather, John McDonald, married a half-Cherokee woman, Ann Shorey, and went to live among his wife's family as a member of the Cherokee tribe. Although Ross himself was only one-eighth Cherokee by blood, he viewed himself as Cherokee rather than white.

As a child, Ross lived in different parts of the Cherokee lands in Georgia and Tennessee, meeting both Indian and white people. He usually dressed in the style of Cherokee boys of that time and played traditional games with his eight brothers and sisters. Ross was very close to his mother, who greatly valued her native heritage. He attended Cherokee ceremonies and celebrations, including the annual spring Green Corn Festival. These were days of plenty, as deer, elk, and game birds roamed Cherokee lands, and both wild and cultivated plants grew in the fertile soil.

During the late 1790s, Ross's parents, Daniel and Mary (Mollie) McDonald Ross, moved to southeastern Tennessee where they built a home near the northern end of Lookout Mountain. Once settled, Daniel Ross set out to educate his children and other Cherokee young people. The Ross home held books and newspapers, and Daniel brought teachers to the region. With his brother Lewis, John Ross attended an academy in Kingston, Tennessee. There, the boys lived with a merchant, working in his store to pay for their room and board. As he completed his schooling, Ross learned much more about whites, their ways of life, and their social institutions.

By that time, the Cherokees had been in contact with whites for nearly 300 years. During the mid-1500s, Spanish explorers had landed on the Florida coast. More whites—fur trappers, traders, and settlers—continued to come to North America. In 1735, about 17,000 Cherokee lived in the Southeast. When an English traveler named William Bartram visited the region in the mid-1700s, he described the Cherokee as "frank, cheerful, and humane . . . tenacious of their liberties and natural rights of man . . . honest, just, and liberal." He said that they moved "with becoming grace and dignity."

As more whites came, conservative Cherokee leaders argued that they should not adopt white ways. Other Cherokee said that they must understand the whites' language and laws in order to keep them from taking control of Cherokee government or lands. During the years before 1776, the British rulers of colonial America did not uphold Native Americans' rights or give them equal benefit of the laws. In 1785 the Cherokee signed a treaty with the new United States. It declared their loyalty and gave them the status of an independent nation, with "inviolable boundaries."

Ross paid close attention when learning about these events as he completed his education and gained business experience. He began taking an active part in tribal politics. He served as a clerk to two of the chiefs. In 1809, at age 19, he was sent by the Indian agent to visit the Arkansas Cherokee (Cherokee who had moved west). Two years later, he became a member of the Standing Committee, a governing panel that made decisions about matters affecting the tribe.

Along with some other Cherokee and some loyal Creek, John Ross served with General Andrew Jackson's Tennessee regiment in the Creek War of 1813–14. The brave Cherokee Regiment played a leading role in Jackson's victory at the Battle of Horseshoe Bend.

When he was 23, John Ross married and established a new home. His wife, Quatie, was a nearly full-blooded Cherokee woman known for her talents and intelligence. In 1814 Ross set up a trading post and ferry service at Ross's Landing on the Tennessee River. His partner was the son of the federal Indian agent whom the Bureau of Indian Affairs had assigned to the Cherokee. To-gether, they worked to get and fulfill contracts from the U.S. government to provide supplies to Indians and soldiers in the region. John Ross gained experience meeting and dealing with various people, skills he later put to use as a tribal leader.

Ross was only 26 years old when he traveled with six other Cherokee leaders to Washington, D.C., to protest the provisions of a treaty, supported by Andrew Jackson, that aimed to take away some Cherokee lands. They were especially offended because they had so recently fought side by side with U.S. troops in the Creek War, sustaining property damage and loss of livestock in the process.

The secretary of war met with the Cherokee and agreed with them, also granting them some money for their losses during the Creek War. The *National Intelligencer* described the Cherokee as "men of cultivation and understanding. Their appearance and deportment are such as to entitle them to respect and attention."

During these years, the Cherokee Nation did get some respect from the U.S. government. They received the diplomatic courtesies given to foreign dignitaries. This was appropriate, since the Cherokee political system was well developed and organized like a govenment, with laws and elected leaders. Council meetings were held to discuss important issues and solve common problems.

Whites brought some changes to the Cherokee's way of life during the early 1800s. Some Indians began to use firearms and metal farm tools that whites brought to the region. Christian missionaries built schools and churches there, urging the Cherokee to learn their religion. Some Cherokee children attended the mission schools. Whites also introduced the idea of slavery—buying and selling black African people who had been forcibly taken from their homelands. (By 1825, there would be about 1,277 black slaves in the Cherokee Nation.)

The Standing Committee became known as the National Committee, and Ross was chosen as its president in 1818. He went to Washington the next year to help draw up the Cherokee Treaty of 1819. For years, different states had been taking Cherokee lands and trying to claim more. There was talk of sending Indians to lands west of the Mississippi River. The Cherokee wanted a guarantee of some permanent lands within their once much-larger territory. They gave up almost 6,000 square miles of land in Tennessee, North Carolina, Alabama, and Georgia during the negotiations. The treaty promised that they could live on the rest of their lands without further intrusion.

For five years, Ross served as president of the National Committee while continuing his business activities. He also acted as captain of the Cherokee Light Horse, a military group that patrolled Cherokee lands, keeping out white trespassers. Ross urged his fellow Cherokee to protest any interference by federal or state officials with their land holdings or with their government.

In the meantime, a Cherokee leader named Sequoyah made a great contribution to his tribe. From 1809 to 1821, he developed a Cherokee alphabet with 86 symbols. The characters of this alphabet stood for the different sounds in the language. This system enabled the Cherokee to read and write in their own language. With this tool, the Cherokee developed tribal newspapers, business papers, and historical records.

Communication among tribe members helped the Cherokee to unite on troublesome issues that continued to confront them. Despite the Treaty of 1819, the U.S. government was now trying to persuade the Cherokee still living in the East—called the Eastern Cherokee—to give up their land. They were offered an equal amount of land in the West and some money for the loss of their property. (The Western Cherokee had accepted a government offer in 1822 and were now living in Arkansas Territory.)

Ross was distressed when he saw the Western Cherokee at their new settlement in 1823. He said they had "suffered severely . . . sickness, wars, and other fatalities have visited them." In a written statement, the Eastern Cherokee refused to move, citing their "love of the soil which gave them birth" and stating that they had firmly decided "never again to cede *one foot* more of land."

By this time, John Ross was known as a hard working, honest leader. In those days, government officials often bribed Native Americans in order to get their cooperation. In 1823 Ross received a letter offering him $2,000 if he would support a new treaty that would remove the Eastern Cherokee. He refused the bribe and later told a Cherokee council, "This letter which I hold in my hand will speak for itself, but fortunately the author of it has mistaken my character and sense of honor."

The struggle over land went on for several years as new Indian agents, assigned by the Bureau of Indian Affairs, came to the region. Many Cherokee resented their presence. Among themselves, they also debated whether to ask for changes in the way the U.S. government made annual payments to Eastern and Western

This photo of Ross shows the Cherokee leader in middle age, shortly after the Cherokee removal to Oklahoma. (Cherokee Nations Communications)

Cherokee for the use of surrendered lands. White settlers continued to violate treaties, so Ross and his committee met with federal officials in Washington to ask their help in dealing with these problems. The Cherokee could not convince U.S. officials to remove the federal Indian agent or punish settlers for violating the treaty, but the whites did agree that Ross was a distinguished representative and negotiator.

After the meeting, Ross realized more than ever that his people must be both united and informed in order to express forceful opinions about matters that affected them. He spearheaded the passage of a law that required the consent of the people, in council meetings, before "acts of a public character," such as land sales, could take place. Ross used some of his own money to revive the *Cherokee Phoenix*, a newspaper written in both Cherokee and English, so that more people would know about tribal concerns.

In 1827 Ross attended a special convention at which the Cherokee formed a unique constitutional form of government. Like the U.S. federal government, the Cherokee system had three main branches: a principal chief and assistant chief, a legislature, and a court system. The tribe agreed that the people would continue to elect their legislators. Chiefs were to be selected by the Cherokee General Council, which elected Ross as principal chief in 1828. He and other leaders hoped that by strengthening and refining their government, the Cherokee would show the United States that their nation was equal in stature to any other. They hoped to have their own state and system of government within the United States.

Meanwhile, Ross, his wife, and their children moved to a two-story house he had built near New Echota, Georgia, the new Cherokee capital. This fine home included kitchens, smokehouses, a basement, and quarters for Ross's field hands, some of whom were slaves. He owned 200 acres, mostly for farming.

The Cherokee's hopes of staying on their lands, as an independent nation, were crushed in 1830. President Andrew Jackson asked the U.S. Congress to pass the Indian Removal Bill. White settlers in the Southeast had urged the government to make more land available by "removing" Native Americans to land located west of the Mississippi River. Over the next eight years, Ross worked to prevent, then delay, the removal of his people. He visited Washington every year and met several times with President Jackson, whom the Cherokees considered their friend.

Although the Cherokee had helped Jackson to win the Creek War, and Ross knew him personally, Jackson refused all pleas to

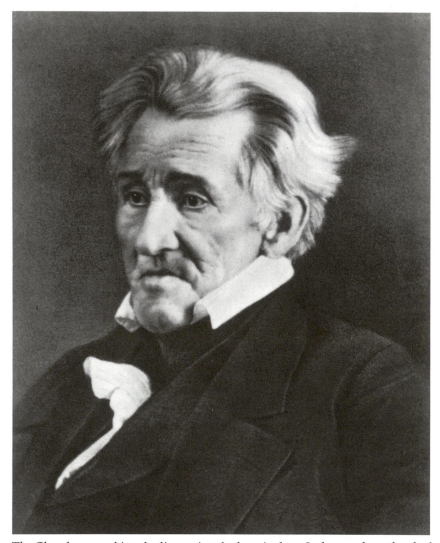

The Cherokee were bitterly disappointed when Andrew Jackson, whom they had aided during the Creek War, upheld state laws that treated them unjustly. (Library of Congress, #13007)

let them stay in the Southeast. As president, Jackson ended annual payments to the Cherokee tribe for the use of their lands. Only individual Indians received money—about 50 cents a person. This caused new hardships, because these annual payments had been the only fixed money the tribe received for its needs.

To complicate matters, gold had been found on Cherokee lands in Georgia. The state assumed control over this land, in some cases giving it to white Georgians. The president and Congress refused to intervene or help the Cherokee. They declared that Georgia had sovereignty—authority—over the people and land within its boundaries.

Working strenuously to get help for his people in Congress and the federal courts, Ross amassed documents, including state laws, maps, old treaties, letters, and tribal resolutions. In most cases he copied these himself and sent them to officials. Some lawmakers, especially those from northeastern states, agreed that the Cherokee had been treated unfairly, but these congressmen did not have enough power to take action.

By corresponding with William Wirt, a former U.S. attorney general, Ross learned the proper procedures for bringing his case through the court system. He and other Cherokee leaders and their lawyers had worked diligently to get the attention of the U.S. Supreme Court. But in 1831, they were devastated when the Court ruled that it had no right to hear the case *Cherokee Nation v. Georgia*. The Court reasoned that the Cherokee were a "domestic dependent nation," not a "foreign state." The next year, another case did reach the U.S. Supreme Court, and Chief Justice John Marshall issued a landmark ruling. He said that Georgia could not pass laws that affected the Cherokee. But the victory turned out to be meaningless, because both President Jackson and Georgia ignored it.

During those years, the federal and state governments and many white citizens urged the removal of the Cherokee. The government promised the Cherokee many benefits if they would move west, but by then, most Cherokee did not trust the government. They did not want to leave their homes, possessions, and way of life, especially in exchange for inferior land. Ross violently opposed removal but saw that his people were being pushed out, step by step. A group of about 500 Cherokee had formed a Treaty Party, in contrast to the anti-treaty or Ross Party. In 1835 the Treaty Party, led by John Ridge and Stand Watie, agreed to the U.S. government's terms for removal and signed the Treaty of New Echota.

Ross and his supporters disagreed with this minority tribal faction. They claimed the Treaty of New Echota was not legal and wrote to Congress in 1836, asking them to examine it. For two more years, Ross worked hard in Washington, now meeting with President Martin Van Buren. He argued that a few Cherokee had no authority to make the 1835 treaty apply to all.

Meanwhile the state of Georgia stripped the anti-treaty Cherokee of their rights, taking their land for unfairly small payments. People stole from the Cherokee without fear of arrest. The *Cherokee Phoenix* was still publishing articles that opposed removal to the West, so some whites destroyed the printing press.

Ross's long struggle ended in heartbreak. In the spring of 1838, he rushed home to Georgia after hearing that troops were rounding up families at gunpoint. They had sent 17,000 Cherokee into camps to await removal. There was not enough clean water or food in the camps and hundreds of Indians died in the over-crowded stockades from dysentery, cholera, whooping cough, and other diseases. A few Cherokee fled and hid in mountain areas, where some of their descendants still live today.

Officials then announced they would transport about 2,500 Cherokee out of the camps. This first group of people were put on boats that traveled along the Tennessee and Mississippi rivers. Their 800-mile journey took all spring and most of the extremely hot, dry summer. Illnesses spread quickly in the crowded boats. Before the Cherokee reached Oklahoma, nearly one-third of them had died from sickness or starvation.

In what must have been the saddest job of his life, John Ross organized the remaining Cherokee for the trip west. Unable to prevent removal, Ross pressed the government for more compensation. The Cherokee formed 13 groups of about 1,000 people each, with conductors, doctors, interpreters, and wagon leaders. The few wagons could accommodate only the sick and very young or very old people; others had to walk much of the 800 miles.

They set out during the rainy autumn of 1838. Winter brought snow and freezing weather. As people died along the way, they fell on the frozen earth. The soldiers rushed people along, not allowing them to bury their dead properly. People later said that these fallen Cherokee were like teardrops on the ground, marking a Trail of Tears to the West.

John Ross's wife was among the victims. Ross and his family left Georgia in November, in the final group of about 228 people. A soldier from North Carolina later said that after Quatie Ross gave "her only Blanket for the protection of a sick child she rode thinly clad through a blinding sleet and snowstorm and developed Pneumonia. . . ." John Ross was able to hire a steamboat to carry his family through the icy rivers to Little Rock, Arkansas. There Quatie died and was buried.

In mid-March, Ross and other survivors arrived in Indian Territory. This group of Cherokee became known as the National Party. From the start, there were conflicts among the various groups. People resented the Treaty Party and its leaders, who had signed the hated Treaty of New Echota. While conflicts and fighting increased among the parties, Ross pleaded for a "war of reason."

Nonetheless, in June 1839, a group of men attacked Treaty Party leader John Ridge while he was sleeping, stabbing him to death. They killed two other party leaders, but Stand Watie escaped. Some Cherokee accused John Ross of taking part in the murders, and his life was threatened, but there was no proof of his involvement.

Cherokee leaders struggled to reunite the tribe and rebuild their nation. Ross had enough followers among the Western Cherokee to be reelected chief in 1839. He helped to set up a new government, the United Cherokee, with a new constitution. Their stated policy was "to live in peace" with other Indian nations and with the government and citizens of the United States, but also to "peaceably seek . . . redress from the scales of justice upheld by the United States."

In December of 1838, President Martin Van Buren had told Congress that the Cherokee "migrated without any apparent reluctance." But other public officials and journalists disagreed emphatically. An eastern newspaper published a letter by a traveler from Maine who had seen the migration. He described the severely cold weather and the illnesses suffered by the Cherokee and said that people had a "downcast, dejected look bordering on . . . despair; others, a wild frantic appearance. . . ." Massachusetts Senator Daniel Webster said "There is a strong and growing feeling in the country that a great wrong has been done to the Cherokee."

Between 1839 and 1846, Ross made six trips to Washington, D.C., to voice the tribe's grievances. The government had broken promises it had made to the Cherokee before they were removed. The costs of their trip and resettlement had far exceeded the federal money they received. People were homeless and lacked farm tools and household goods, having been forced to leave things behind. In 1842 Ross wrote to the secretary of war, "I do hereby most solemnly protest against this unprecedented violation of that sacred rule . . . of treating with all due respect those who had ever presented themselves under a flag of truce."

In 1844 a new newspaper, the *Cherokee Advocate*, was started, with articles in English and Cherokee. Its motto—"Our Rights—Our Country—Our Race"—showed the tribe's unquenchable spirit and will to rebuild. The United Cherokee developed a public education system with schools for both men and women, something Ross had advocated. This plan showed advanced thinking, because white society did not then view women as intellectually equal to men.

Before the removal west, Ross had packed his copies of treaties and tribal documents to take with him. When, in 1857, the U.S. government made plans to sell property it had promised to the Cherokee, Ross was able to show the Indian commissioner a treaty that proved his position. As a result, the property was returned to the tribe.

John Ross had remarried, choosing a Quaker, Mary Bryan Stapler, and had succeeded in rebuilding his fortune, with a plantation in Indian Territory and slaves he had brought from Georgia. The issue of slavery, debated by Americans during the mid-1800s, also divided the Cherokee. By 1860 they had about 4,000 slaves, but a number of Cherokee believed slavery was wrong.

When the Civil War broke out in 1861, the Cherokee were likewise split over which side to support—the North, or Union side, which opposed slavery, or the Confederacy of southern states that refused to end slavery. At first, John Ross urged his tribe to stay neutral. Then he joined Stand Watie and other powerful Cherokee who supported the South. Some historians think he may have changed his position to avoid further intertribal conflict.

By fall 1862 the Confederacy had lost ground, and Union troops gained control in Indian Territory. Ross moved his family to Kansas. When he met with Union officials at Fort Smith, Arkansas, they asked the Cherokee to grant railroad rights across Cherokee land and pledge their loyalty to the Union. Agreeing, Ross again changed his allegiance, but, by then, people disagreed over who was the true Cherokee leader. Stand Watie, now a general in the Confederate Army, had been elected chief by supporters who called themselves the Southern Cherokee. They did not join Ross and the Western Cherokee in supporting the Union before the war ended in 1865.

During these difficult years, Ross had reached his seventies and lay ill, bedridden, much of the time. He carried on through correspondence and the help of supporters. A new Cherokee treaty, declaring Ross as principal chief of the whole tribe, was finally worked out in July 1866. But, on August 1, John Ross died while on another diplomatic mission to Washington, D.C.

Ross had struggled valiantly to help his people during a devastating era. He had faced powerful officials who used conflicts within the tribe to weaken the Cherokee before and after their removal. Yet through the years, Ross had repeatedly united opposing groups so they could work for the common good. In doing so, he had made difficult choices, balancing the needs of his people against outside pressures from white officials.

In some cases, Ross's knowledge and bargaining skills had enabled him to gain fairer treatment for his people. John Ross always tried to do his best, even when the Cherokee lost disputes. He refused to accept terms that let the government meet only the minimum treaty requirements. Much of the progress the Cherokee made after their removal, in forming a united government and in educating themselves, came through his work. And though many of Ross's pleas for justice were ignored, he inspired others, including

John Ross during his later years. At his death in 1866, Ross was considered principal chief of the faction of Cherokee he had tried so hard to unite. (©Smithsonian Institution, neg. #988a)

some whites, to urge fairer treatment for Native Americans in the years that followed. As his nephew, William P. Ross, said at his funeral, John Ross "would send an influence far down the stream of time."

WASHAKIE

◆ ◆ ◆

Quest for a New Shoshone Homeland

The mid-1800s were grim years for the Plains Indians. Gold deposits had been found on their lands, and miners surged west, joining thousands of other white settlers. Washakie, respected leader of the Wind River Shoshone of Wyoming, arrived at Fort Laramie in 1851 on horseback for yet another treaty meeting with white officials and Indian leaders. For 18 days, Washakie described the struggles of his people to keep their hunting grounds and way of life.

Despite his efforts, once again, Shoshone land was cut up and reduced. Diplomatically, Washakie told officials, "I have come a great distance to see you . . . and I am glad and my people are glad we have come. Our hearts are full; all our hearts are full of your words. We will talk them over again." Still hopeful of fair treatment from the whites whom the Shoshone had regarded as friends, Washakie headed back to his camp. Like other leaders, he faced a terrible dilemma: whether to fight or come to distasteful terms with the whites. And what chance would his people have if they fought? For Washakie had known since his youth that these intruders had "superior tools and terrible weapons."

◆ ◆ ◆

Named *Pina Quahah* ("sweet smelling") at birth, the future leader was born to a Wind River (Eastern) Lemhi-Shoshone mother. His father, Paseego, had Flathead, Umatilla, and Shoshone heritage. His birthdate was probably between 1798 and 1804.

Like Black Kettle of the Cheyenne, Washakie was born around the time of the Louisiana Purchase and the subsequent Lewis and Clark expedition across North America. During the fall and winter of 1804–05, Lewis and Clark camped in Mandan villages along the Missouri River and asked about other tribes that lived on their route west. The explorers had heard that the Shoshone bred outstanding horses, and they hoped to buy some for their journey.

The group camped at the Three Forks area near the Missouri River in present-day Montana. By then, as Meriwether Lewis wrote in his diary, "we began to feel considerable anxiety . . . if we do not find [the Shoshone] or some other nation who have horses I fear the successful issue of our voyage will be doubtful. . . ."

Lewis led a party that set out to find the tribe, killing elk and deer along the way for food. On August 11, 1805, they saw an Indian, whom Lewis said "was mounted on an elegant horse without a saddle, and a small string which was attached to the under jaw of the horse which answered as a bridle." Later, the explorers visited a Shoshone camp, where they passed out beads and mirrors as gestures of friendship.

Next, Clark's group arrived. In his party was the Shoshone woman Sacajawea, who was serving as guide and interpreter for the expedition. She expressed excitement and delight upon finding that these people were members of her native tribe. The Shoshone fed the travelers and furnished them with horses, and with information they needed to continue their journey.

During this time, Washakie was living with his father's tribe in the Bitterroot Mountains of present-day Montana. When his father died during a Blackfoot raid on the village, his mother took him and his two brothers and two sisters to live with her people in western Wyoming. This band of Shoshone lived near the Wind River Mountains, which are part of the Rockies.

During his youth, Washakie spent a few years among the Bannock, a group that spoke a similar language, also from Salish roots.

Tall and strong, he distinguished himself in battles against enemy Indians. Several other tribes—Cheyenne, Arapaho, Crow, Blackfoot, and Sioux—competed with the Shoshone for good buffalo hunting grounds. The Shoshone of Wyoming and Montana were chiefly hunters, while the Shoshone who lived around the Snake River of Idaho hunted and also fished for salmon.

Washakie returned to his own group a respected warrior. At that time, he was sometimes called "scar face," because of the deep scar on his left cheek, the result of a Blackfoot arrow. He supposedly got the name *Washakie* after killing his first bison. After skinning the bison's head and removing the hair, he tied the skin around a stick. Then he blew the skin up like a balloon and put stones inside. It dried into a sort of rattle that he carried into battle and used as a noisemaker to startle the enemy or to stampede herds of horses during a raid. The name *Washakie* means "the rattle" or "gourd rattle."

But his rattle was not the only unusual thing about Washakie. He was also physically striking—he stood over six feet tall, and people who met him often commented on his elegant posture. He was also a talented singer, and used the rattle to accompany himself. Other Shoshone admired his arrow-making skills and the strong bows he made from elk horns, strengthened with sinew—animal tendon—and coats of pitch from pine trees. He decorated elk skins with intricate paintings.

Respected by his tribespeople, Washakie also made friends among whites, starting with the fur trappers who came to Shoshone lands. As a boy, he earned money by herding ponies for a group of trappers two years in a row. He once told a white friend, Nelson Yarnell, "My first experience with them was so pleasant I had determined to go [back]."

The trappers brought Washakie a gun, something he had wanted very much. Owning a gun further increased his prestige among his people, and Washakie later claimed, "All the young men of my tribe followed me, because I could shoot further than they." He told the trappers that in the future he would avoid war with white men, and would also try to keep his people out of such wars.

As trading posts sprang up among the Indians, they became more dependent on white trade for goods, such as guns, ammunition, tools, cloth, metal cookware, and ornaments. Washakie and other Shoshone trapped beaver to trade for such goods. During the 1820s and 1830s, he made friends with some of the famous mountain men of the era, including Kit Carson and James Bridger. Washakie took part in the yearly meetings, called *rendezvous*, where these men got together.

By the 1840s, the beaver population had declined and the trappers had to go further west in the search for furs. With fewer guns available, the Shoshone had more problems defending themselves against the Sioux and Cheyenne.

Washakie had become a tribal leader by then. Chief Padashawaunda had led the Shoshone for several years. When his brother, Mowoomhah, became chief, Washakie and two others served as minor chiefs. Around this time, Washakie also married. During his lifetime, it is thought that he was married three or four times and had 12 children. One wife was a Shoshone woman, while another was a Crow named Ahawhypersie. Two daughters' names have been recorded as Enga Peahroa and Naunangai; his four sons were Cocoosh (Dick Washakie), Connayah (Bishop Washakie), Wobaah (Charles Washakie), and George Washakie.

Although Washakie had not fought against white settlers or soldiers, he continued to be a fierce warrior against Shoshone enemies. According to trapper and journalist Osborne Russell, Washakie and the two minor chiefs were "the pillars of the nation at whose names the Blackfeet quaked with fear."

After Chief Mowoomhah died in the late 1840s, the tribe became divided over many issues. Washakie was elected chief at this difficult time. He had shown courage, wisdom, speaking skills, unselfishness—traits that often led to leadership positions in a tribe. After becoming chief, Washakie moved his people to a new camp on the Green River in southwestern Wyoming. Seeking to form a safer, larger group, other Shoshone bands joined them and treated Washakie as their leader. The group stretched from the North Platte and Wind rivers to the Great Salt Lake in Utah.

In keeping with the promise he had made years earlier, Washakie told his followers not to attack or steal from wagon trains moving westward to Oregon. More whites were coming each year, and the religious group called Mormons established a settlement at the Great Salt Lake, the southern part of his tribe's hunting grounds.

During these years, many Indians died in fights with whites, but Washakie helped his people to avoid much of this tragedy. Under his leadership, the Shoshone formed patrols of young men who helped the whites cross difficult terrain and rivers and recover stray animals. Washakie befriended Mormon leader Brigham Young, even though the Mormons also traded with his tribe's enemies, the Ute.

As more settlers and gold miners came west during the 1850s, the U.S. War Department set up forts along their major routes in Idaho, Nebraska, and Wyoming. At one time, the government had planned to send all Native Americans to a large area in the West designated as Indian Territory; now, officials decided to disperse tribes on smaller reservations throughout the West.

In 1851 Washakie joined Sioux, Cheyenne, Ute, and Arapaho leaders at Fort Laramie for the treaty conference described at the beginning of this chapter. Some Cheyenne attacked the Shoshone as they approached the fort. One hostile Sioux also rode forward, claiming that Washakie had once killed a member of his family. These conflicts had to be resolved before the meeting could begin.

The Shoshone were disappointed with the treaty that resulted from the 18 days of talks. It allocated the northern Plains to the Sioux, Arapaho, Crow, and four other tribes. Included with the Crows' land was a northeastern hunting area between the Powder River and Wind River Mountains long used by the Shoshone. Unhappy with these terms, Washakie worked to strengthen his ties with the Mormons. Brigham Young had been named Indian superintendent for the Utah region in 1850, and he tried to stay friendly with both the Ute and the Shoshone. Washakie wanted Young to return the hunting lands between the Wind and Powder rivers that had been given to the Crow.

Washakie (Shoots-the-Buffalo-Running) is shown here seated holding a pipe. Even in his later years, Washakie impressed the younger tribe members with his hunting skills. (National Archives #129)

Young sent traders and missionaries into Shoshone villages. Washakie's people liked trading but did not welcome the missionaries. James S. Brown gave Washakie a copy of his church's religious text, *The Book of Mormon*, but Washakie replied that it was not right for his people. He forbade Shoshone women to marry Mormons, as Young had urged, fearing whites would gain too much influence in the tribe.

Unlike some other Plains Indian leaders, Washakie was open-minded about farming. He saw that the population of game was declining, along with the Shoshone's hunting grounds. They would need to look to other ways to support and feed themselves. He himself did not farm, but he encouraged other men to learn from the Mormons. Bazil, a subchief and the adopted son of Sacajawea, raised wheat and corn along the Green River, according to Mormon John Brown, who wrote about these events in *Life of a Pioneer*.

The friendship between Mormons and Shoshone diminished in 1857 when the Mormon War started. The Mormons clashed with settlers of other Protestant faiths who began settling in Utah. These settlers objected to polygamy (plural marriage) and other Mormon customs. More U.S. military troops came to Utah to keep peace, and President James Buchanan dismissed Young as the governor of Utah. The Mormons left the Shoshone on the Green River, retreating to Zion, the chief Mormon settlement.

Brigham Young asked the Ute and Shoshone to join him in fighting federal troops, but Washakie decided it would be unwise to side against the U.S. government. During the winter of 1857–58, Washakie met the new Indian agent, Dr. Jacob Forney, and assured him that the Shoshone would not fight U.S. troops. He asked Forney for a Shoshone homeland in the Warm Valley, then occupied by the Crow. With a good water supply and natural barriers against harsh weather, this valley would enable his people to raise crops and animals.

In 1861 an Indian agency just for the Shoshone was set up at Fort Bridger. But by then, more settlers were coming west by a new route along the Sweetwater to the Snake River, on Shoshone and Bannock hunting areas. Their presence disturbed the game animals. Some angry young warriors began raiding immigrant parties in 1862.

By then, the United States was embroiled in the Civil War, but some troops were sent west to stop the violence. Fort Halleck was built near Elk Mountain, Wyoming, to protect settlers traveling on the Overland Trail. Soldiers from California came to the region and attacked some Indian villages known for being unfriendly to whites. Colonel Patrick E. Connor led a campaign against a group of northwestern Shoshone led by Bear Hunter. During a battle near the Bear River in Idaho, more than 200 Indians were killed.

Washakie had maintained all along that his people could not defeat the whites in a war. He protected his band by taking them to Fort Bridger until the fighting died down in 1863. That year, Washakie signed a new peace treaty that let travelers pass safely through Shoshone territory in exchange for $20,000 each year for twenty years. (Later, the Senate reduced it to 10 years.) The money was meant to help compensate the Shoshone for lost land and game. About $6,000 worth of goods, mainly food and clothing, were given to the group after the treaty was signed.

Washakie had kept his people's trust as he guided them through these trying years. His prestige rose even higher as he managed to get money and material goods they needed to survive. The chief had not given up his hope of moving from the Green River to Warm Valley. The Shoshone had joined with the Crow to oppose enemy Sioux, who were causing problems for U.S. army engineers trying to open a road north from the Platte River to the mining areas of Montana.

In June 1868 Washakie, still a vigorous leader in his sixties, met with a federal official at Fort Bridger. He asked for a Shoshone reservation at Wind River in present-day Wyoming. His people were willing to exchange the Green River area for the more fertile lands the Shoshone thought were rightfully theirs. Shortly thereafter, Washakie signed the Treaty of Fort Bridger, which permitted Union Pacific Railroad telegraph lines to cross Shoshone lands. Washakie agreed that his band would move to Wind River Reservation, giving up claims to other lands in Utah and Wyoming.

George Washakie (reclining) is shown with a group of Shoshone and Arapaho in front of J. K. Moore's trader's store in Fort Washakie, Wyoming Territory. The photo was taken in August 1883. Back row, left to right: Cammache, Ute Bob, Wallowing Bull, Ground Bear, Sage, Black Coal. Front row: Nam-ma-gan-na-dza, a visiting Idaho Shoshone, Ah-Quita's son, Jim Washakie, Nacoita. (Photo by F. Jay Haynes, Haynes Foundation Collection, Montana Historical Society, Helena, MT)

Washakie had worked for years to obtain this reservation on ancestral lands. It extended over more than three million acres and included good natural resources. The government allocated $20,000 to erect a school and agency buildings. Each head of a household was entitled to 320 acres for an individual farm and $100 worth of seeds and tools to start, as well as $25 for each of the following three years to buy needed farm supplies.

Unfortunately, hostile bands of Cheyenne, Arapaho, and Sioux set out to keep the Shoshone from their reservation by attacking their camps in north-central Wyoming. The U.S. military set up Camp Augur (later Camp Brown) near the Wind River reservation to stop the violence. Meanwhile, miners were settling on the southern part of the reservation. Upset by these events, Washakie moved his people to Utah in 1871, then to Camp Brown in Wyoming. Federal officials promised military aid but asked the Shoshone to give up some of their southern lands. Since there was little game or water there, Washakie agreed to compromise again, in exchange for $25,000, to be paid over a five-year period.

After this 1872 agreement, Washakie wanted to move to the reservation and build up a cattle herd. The Shoshone were still having trouble with hostile tribes. In 1874 soldiers helped them repel raiders and horse thieves on their land.

A group of Shoshone joined with Bannock and Ute warriors to fight on the side of federal troops during the Sioux War of 1876. Washakie returned to the reservation in August 1876, but two of his sons stayed on, leading a band of 100 warriors who helped the government troops fight hostile Indians. In 1878 Washakie's warriors rode with Colonel Ranald S. Mackenzie against Dull Knife's Cheyenne, near the Big Horn Mountains. The fighting finally ended the next spring, as the Sioux leader Crazy Horse surrendered. Another great Sioux leader, Sitting Bull, took his people to Canada.

After subduing hostile Plains tribes, the government sent the tribes to different reservations—the Sioux to the Dakotas and the Cheyenne to Indian Territory. Nearly a thousand Arapaho were assigned to share the Wind River reservation with the Shoshone, despite Washakie's objections. Once again, the U.S. government had abandoned its promise to keep whites and other Indians off Shoshone land. Federal agents did build a school and some flour mills on the reservation. In 1875 the tribe also received some 5,000 head of cattle. Despite this help, many of the Shoshone had trouble adjusting to this new way of life.

In honor of the chief's help and loyalty, Camp Brown was renamed Camp Washakie in 1878. Washakie received a silver medal and a silver-mounted saddle from President Ulysses S. Grant. His response to these gifts showed one of the ways Indians saw themselves as different from whites: "Do a kindness to a [white man], he feels it in his head and his tongue speaks; do a kindness to an Indian, he feels it in his heart. The heart has no tongue."

The last known photo of Washakie, taken at Fort Washakie in 1892. Washakie is standing and pointing. (National Archives #73)

In 1883 Chief Washakie welcomed President Chester Alan Arthur during the president's fishing trip to Yellowstone National Park. During his more than 80 years, Washakie had lived through many historical events. He was moved to paint a series of elk skins

President Chester Alan Arthur was among the white officials who respected Washakie as a leader. The two men met during the president's 1883 vacation at Yellowstone Park. (Library of Congress #13021)

that illustrated his recollections of battles, hunts, and tribal ceremonies.

Chief Washakie signed his last treaty in 1896. It gave the U.S. government about 10 square miles of land in exchange for $60,000. During his nineties, Washakie was often ill. By 1899, he was blind and his legs were nearly paralyzed. Younger men had taken his place as leaders. Still, Washakie made his opinions known and stressed traditional dances and ways among his people.

He was still considered a member of the U.S. Army when he died in 1900 at Flathead Village in Montana's Bitterroot Valley. Washakie was buried with full military honors at the Fort Washakie cemetery.

In 1878 Washakie had met with John W. Hoyt, governor of Wyoming Territory, in order to "speak freely of the many wrongs we have suffered at the hands of the white man." His words convey the plight and feelings of many other Indians during the 1800s:

> The white man, who possesses this whole vast country from sea to sea, who roams over it at pleasure and lives where he likes, cannot know the cramp we feel in this little spot, with the enduring remembrance of the fact, which you know as well as we, that every foot of what you proudly call America, not very long ago belonged to the red man. The Great Spirit gave it to us. There was room enough for all his many tribes, and we all were happy in their freedom.

Few Indian tribes had been as hospitable to whites as the Shoshone of Wyoming. As a leader of these mounted (horse-owning) Indians, Washakie saved many lives by keeping his people out of conflicts with soldiers and settlers, and through tireless negotiations and compromises, he was able to obtain a good-sized reservation on their original lands. A practical leader, Washakie saw early on the futility of going to war against numerous armed white troops. He was continually challenged by new Indian agents, by changing government policies, and by the need to learn new ways of surviving. Yet Washakie guided his people as they moved from one settlement to another and learned to farm and raise cattle. One of his greatest achievements was in being able to make friends with white officials while still being trusted by his own people.

BLACK KETTLE

◆ ◆ ◆

Betrayal of a Peace Chief

On November 29, 1864, an encampment of about 500 peaceful Cheyenne, under their chief, Black Kettle, were the victims of one of the most hideous massacres in U.S. history. Colonel John Chivington led some 1,000 armed soldiers to surround Black Kettle's camp at daybreak. Without provocation, Chivington ordered his troops to attack. Ignoring the white flag of truce and the American flag waving above Black Kettle's tipi, soldiers began firing with rifles and cannon. Chivington then ordered his men to "kill and scalp all, big and little. . . . Nits grow into lice."

The Indian men tried to defend the camp as others, mostly women and children, fled to a creek bed, hoping they would be safe. But soldiers chased after these unarmed Indians and murdered them. Witnesses later described the atrocities. Lieutenant James D. Connor testified, "In going over the battleground the next day, I did not see a body of man, woman, or child but was scalped and in many instances their bodies were mutilated in the most horrible manner. . . ." Another lieutenant reported, "Our force was so large that there was no necessity of firing on the Indians. They did not return the fire until after our troops had fired several rounds . . . I told Colonel Chivington that it would be murder, in every sense of the word."

Chief Black Kettle and a few others managed to escape the slaughter, which became known as the Sand Creek Massacre. For years, he had struggled to negotiate a treaty that would allow his small band to live in peace. After the massacre, Black Kettle would keep trying, but again, he would be betrayed.

◆ ◆ ◆

The tumultuous events that nearly destroyed the Southern Cheyenne began to unfold during the early 1800s, when Moketavato, later called Black Kettle, was a child. The exact year is not known, although his nephew, George Bent, claimed it was 1807. Black Kettle may have been the son of Chief High-Backed Wolf, or of Swift Hawk Lying Down, who was not a chief.

For thousands of years before his birth, Black Kettle's people, the Cheyenne, lived in present-day Minnesota. During the late 1670s, they left their eastern woodland homes and eventually settled in the western Plains of South Dakota and Wyoming, according to Cheyenne tribal historian Black Moccasin. In 1680 the French explorer Rene Robert Cavelier met a group of Cheyenne along the Illinois River. These people called themselves *Tsis tsis tas*, meaning "similarly bred." But French traders gave them the name *Cheyenne*, possibly from a Sioux word *Sha hi ena*, or "language not understood."

At that time, the people lived in earth lodges, but they changed to tipis made of skins as they began to follow and hunt buffalo. Such hunts became easier after the tribe obtained horses around 1740. By the 1800s, the Cheyenne were respected and feared for their skills as horsemen and as warriors.

In 1803, President Thomas Jefferson signed the Louisiana Purchase, an agreement by which the United States paid France for land between the Mississippi River and the Rocky Mountains. France claimed that it had conquered and now owned this land, although numerous Native American tribes had lived there for centuries. After paying France, the United States considered itself the new owner. The claims of Indians, including the Cheyenne, were overlooked and ignored.

Jefferson sent American explorers, led by Meriwether Lewis and William Clark, to the West so they could bring back reports about the land and the native peoples. In 1804, they met some

Cheyenne who were visiting a Mandan village that lay across their route to the Pacific. Clark visited one Cheyenne chief in his lodge made of 20 buffalo skins and offered him a medal. But, as Clark wrote in his journal, the chief gave it back "and informed me that the white people were all *medecine** and that he was afraid of the midal or any thing that white people gave to them." The chief later accepted it when Clark explained to him that the medal was a sincere token to be given from the Great Father—the president—to great chiefs who met with the men in the expedition. The chief fed the travelers, giving Clark "a trencher of boiled corn and beans to eat (as is the custom of all the Nations on the Missouri to give something to every white man who enters their lodge . . .)."

During Black Kettle's youth, the Cheyenne mistrusted whites and were reluctant to mingle with them. The idea that the white men's objects contained dangerous "medicine," or power, had circulated for decades. Years before Lewis and Clark arrived, a French trader had given a Cheyenne leader some gifts; afterward, three of the leader's children died from sickness. Besides, an old Cheyenne prophecy predicted that misfortune would befall the tribe after associating with white-skinned strangers. For these reasons, the Cheyenne as a group avoided spending time with whites. Attitudes gradually changed as some Cheyenne made friends with white fur trappers and traded with them during the early 1800s.

Not much is known about Black Kettle's life during these years. As a young man, he was said to have been a fine scout and brave warrior who fought against the Ute, the Delaware, and other enemy tribes. During the 1820s, his family may have lived near the mouth of the Teton River.

In 1832 the Cheyenne split into two groups, the Southern and Northern Cheyenne. The entire tribe had been living around the Cheyenne River near the Black Hills of present-day South Dakota and Wyoming. Some Cheyenne were drawn by the warmer climate to spend winters in what is now Colorado, at the southern edge of the Rockies. Others went to that region to raid settlements for horses or to hunt for beaver and bear. As more Cheyenne

*power

settled there, they developed into a separate group, the Southern Cheyenne. Black Kettle's family was part of this group.

At that time, relations with whites were fairly calm. Cheyenne patronized trading posts, such as Bent's Fort in the southern area. William Bent, owner of the trading post, had married Owl Woman, daughter of a Cheyenne holy man. At the fort, Black Kettle and other Indians traded for metal pots and pans, belt buckles, knives, guns, axes, cloth, blankets, and foods such as sugar, flour, coffee, tea, bread, eggs, and spices.

The Southern Cheyenne had traditionally been enemies with the Comanche, Pawnee, and Kiowa. Their allies were the Arapaho, a Plains tribe that had also come long ago from the eastern woodlands and spoke a form of Algonquian, as did the Cheyenne. The 1830s were troublesome years for Plains Indians. Whites brought diseases such as cholera, measles, and smallpox, which were new to them and to which they had little resistance. Whites also brought guns and alcohol. Guns enabled Indians to kill their enemies more quickly in battle. Alcohol, something Indians were also not used to, damaged their health and communities. Sometimes whites tried to make Indians drunk, then tricked them into taking less money for the trading goods, such as furs.

By the 1840s, the Southern Cheyenne had made peace with some of their former enemies, except for the Ute, who lived in present-day Colorado. During an 1848 battle against the Ute, Black Kettle's first wife was captured. He was married again, to a woman who belonged to the Wotapio band of Cheyenne. By 1853, his tribe respected him enough to give him the honor of carrying the sacred Medicine Arrows into a battle against the Delaware Indians.

Fighting among Indians worried white farmers and ranchers, as well as miners who had come there to search for gold. In 1851 the government urged the major Plains tribal leaders to attend a council meeting in southeastern Colorado, where they were asked to sign a treaty.

Black Kettle and other leaders on horseback led thousands of Cheyenne and other bands to the meeting. They set up tipis around Fort Laramie and held feasts to honor each other, serving boiled buffalo tongue, roasted buffalo rib, and edible wild plants. The

Cheyenne displayed their horsemanship and entertained onlookers with a war dance that dramatized heroic past deeds.

At the meeting, the U.S. government told Black Kettle, through interpreters, that it would set boundaries on Cheyenne lands. Cheyenne-Arapaho territory was to be located within an area bordered by the North Platte River on the north, the Arkansas River on the south, along through western Kansas in the east and up to the Rocky Mountains in the west. Black Kettle felt he had no choice but to sign the Treaty of Fort Laramie, which the whites promised to honor. He was praised for being a great peace chief during these negotiations.

Yet Black Kettle's band faced added problems as more whites came west. In 1853 alone, 15,000 whites passed through Bent's Fort. Besides bringing more epidemics, whites hunted on Indian lands and offended them in other ways. The Cheyenne and other Plains Indians retaliated by raiding settlements. By 1857 Colonel E. V. Sumner was leading the U.S. army in large-scale attacks on the Cheyenne to demonstrate the government's control in the region.

In 1860 the Southern Cheyenne and some Arapaho agreed to move to a reservation located north of the Arkansas River. Records show that Chief Black Kettle signed this agreement, along with chiefs White Antelope, Lean Bear, Little Wolf, Tall Bear, and Left Hand. The government promised that whites would not be allowed to live on these lands and that the tribes would receive food, clothing, tools, and other goods as payment for the land they had lost. But the reservation was too dry for farming and was poor for hunting. To make matters worse, the government did not send the goods it had promised, although Black Kettle and other leaders met with officials numerous times.

During the Civil War years (1861–65), more settlers were eager to move west. New U. S. Army forts were built along the trails to protect them. By 1861 Black Kettle's band desperately needed food, clothing, and other goods. He traveled to Fort Lyon, later Fort Wise, Colorado, near Bent's Trading Post. (George Bent, William's son, had married one of Black Kettle's nieces.) Black Kettle asked the fort commander for food and supplies. Although

This group of Cheyenne and Arapaho chiefs negotiated with U.S. officials when they were sent to a joint reservation. Front row, left to right: One-Eye, Black Kettle (holding pipe), Bull Bear, White Antelope. Back row, order uncertain: Neva, Heap O' Buffaloes, No-ta-nee (Knock Knee). (Archives and Manuscript Division of the Oklahoma Historical Society)

the fort was also short of goods, the commander gave the Cheyenne enough to prevent an uprising.

In February of that same year, Black Kettle attended another treaty session at Fort Wise. Again, he signed an agreement, this one binding all parties to keep peace in Colorado and along the Santa Fe Trail. The Treaty of Fort Wise was later criticized by some of the chiefs who had signed and by others who refused. An Arapaho chief, Little Raven, expressed their frustration and noted the ongoing problems Indians had when negotiating with whites.

He said, "The Cheyennes signed it first, then I. But we did not know what it was. That is one reason why I want an interpreter, so that I can know what I sign."

On behalf of his people, Black Kettle made several visits to Washington, D.C., as part of Indian treaty delegations. One such delegation, in 1863, included Lean Bear, War Bonnet, and Standing in the Water. The Cheyenne asked President Abraham Lincoln to make sure that treaty promises were kept. Lincoln said he hoped that past treaties would be honored. But the president was preoccupied with the Civil War, and the treatment of Indians varied in different regions, often depending on the types of army leaders there.

Peace seemed ever more remote as Indians and settlers fought in Colorado. Black Kettle went to Denver in 1864, again asking for protection from white trespassers, but Governor John Evans wanted to open more Indian hunting grounds to white settlers. Colonel John Chivington, known for being hostile to Indians, led the state militia in a campaign against the Cheyenne and Arapaho. Under his orders, troops attacked the Cheyenne as punishment for raids on white settlements.

Not all army officers mistreated Indians. Sensing trouble ahead, Major T. I. McKenney said,

> I think if great caution is not exercised on our part, there will be a bloody war. It should be our policy to try and conciliate them, guard our mails and trains well to prevent theft, and stop these scouting parties that are roaming over the country, who do not know one tribe from another and who will kill anything in the shape of an Indian. It will require only a few more murders on the part of our troops to unite all these warlike tribes.

In May of 1864, the violence McKenney had dreaded came to pass. Lieutenant George S. Eyre's troops found Chief Lean Bear and other Cheyenne hunting buffalo north of Fort Larned. Lean Bear rode forward, showing the medal and letter he had received from President Lincoln, vouching that he was trustworthy.

Eyre's soldiers ignored his peaceful overtures and shot Lean Bear and his companions in cold blood. Enraged, Cheyenne raided wagon trains and settlements, while U.S. soldiers retaliated by burning Indian villages and stealing their horses. This conflict became known as the Cheyenne-Arapaho War, or Colorado War, of 1864–65.

With the help of George Bent, Black Kettle and other peace chiefs wrote a letter in August 1865 asking for an end to the fighting. Black Kettle knew that the whites had more military power than his people. At a council at Camp Weld outside Denver, the Indians reached an agreement with Governor Evans. Their bands could remain safe by camping near army posts, without fear of being attacked, so long as they kept in touch with the fort commander regularly, said the governor.

Black Kettle doubted whether Evans would keep his promise, but his people had few choices. He led about 600 Southern Cheyenne and Arapaho followers to Fort Lyon that November. Black Kettle told the commander they had come in peace. Unfortunately, a new commander had replaced Major Edward Wynkoop, whom Black Kettle knew and trusted. The Indians were told to return to their nearby camp at Sand Creek.

The new fort commander, Major Scott Anthony, assembled troops armed with rifles. Anthony had often expressed contempt for Indians and he asked Colonel Chivington to join him with his Colorado Third Regiment, called the Bloodless Third because they had never seen battle. The men in this regiment were eager to overcome their reputation for weakness.

On November 29, 1864, Anthony and Chivington led about 1,000 men, many of them drunk, to surround Black Kettle's camp and attack the peaceful Indians with rifles and cannon. Black Kettle and some warriors fought from behind a high bank, then managed to escape. Chiefs White Antelope and Yellow Wolf were among the 400–500 dead. White Antelope had walked forward with his hand high, a sign of surrender, asking the soldiers not to shoot. They killed him without provocation.

The U.S. Congress investigated and condemned Colonel Chivington's actions at Sand Creek, calling them an "outrage . . . gross and wanton," and he had to resign. Yet this massacre infuriated many Plains Indians and made them distrust whites even more. The Cheyenne had relied on promises made by the government, but the white men contradicted each other and did not honor their treaties.

Despite his ordeals, Black Kettle still hoped for peace. But many young Cheyenne chose to follow more militant leaders, including the famous war chief Roman Nose. Militant Southern Arapaho rallied behind Little Raven and Left Hand. The Sand Creek Massacre, having pushed so many Indians to feel that war was the only answer, sparked conflicts between the whites and Plains Indians that were to continue until the massacre at Wounded Knee, South Dakota, in 1890, effectively ended the Plains Indian wars.

Government officials called for a new peace council in 1865. Black Kettle signed the Treaty of Little Arkansas at the meeting, held near present-day Wichita, Kansas. As the council began, the chief spoke eloquently about the Cheyenne's hopes and concerns. Revealing his deep frustration, he said, "I once thought that I was the only man that persevered to be the friend of the white man, but since they have come and [robbed] our lodges, horses, and everything else, it is hard for me to believe the white men any more." A white journalist, J. R. Mead, wrote in the *Wichita Eagle* that Chief Black Kettle was "mild, peaceable, pleasant, and good."

Major Wynkoop invited Black Kettle to a meeting in 1867 where Southern Cheyenne signed the Treaty of Medicine Lodge. It relocated the Cheyenne to a reservation in Indian Territory (now Oklahoma). By this time, the transcontinental railroad was moving relentlessly across America and onto Cheyenne land, driving away the buffalo with its noise and bringing many new settlers. Black Kettle was trying to be practical but firm in his struggle to reach a peaceful agreement with the U.S. government.

Other Cheyenne who did not agree with that philosophy continued to conduct raids in Kansas and other places, so settlers asked for more protection. In Kansas, General Philip H. Sheridan sent out a small, mobile force of 50 soldiers to locate Indian warriors who were causing trouble. However, the Cheyenne were able to elude Sheridan's group. He continued to attack Plains Indians, in what became known as the Sheridan Campaign of 1868–69.

The Treaty of Medicine Lodge proved to be yet another bitter disappointment for Black Kettle. Whites moved onto the reservation lands, and some rebel bands of Cheyenne attacked them. For safety's sake, Black Kettle took his band to stay among the Kiowa in winter camps in northwestern Indian Territory. Seeing the dire needs of the Cheyenne, the Kiowa offered them new horses and fully stocked lodges to live in.

Black Kettle then led his people to the upper Washita River in Indian Territory. Hoping to avoid war, he traveled with a Cheyenne chief, Little Robe, and some Arapaho leaders 75 miles south to Fort Cobb. There he told Colonel William B. Hazen,

> I have always done my best to keep the young men quiet, but some will not listen and since the fighting began, I have not been able to keep them all at home. But we all want peace, and I would be glad to move my people down this way. I could then keep them all quietly near camp.

Before an arrangement was reached, Colonel George Armstrong Custer discovered the Cheyenne camp at Washita. One year earlier, Custer had been humiliated during his failed campaign against some Plains Indians. Custer marched his Seventh Cavalry across the snowy prairie, and at dawn on November 27, 1868, they attacked the Cheyenne camp.

Through the cold morning fog, Black Kettle saw the "bluecoats" coming. He and his wife rode forward to talk with the men, but without warning, both were shot and killed. Black Kettle, ever hopeful, was holding the American flag in his hand as he fell from his horse.

The cavalry then attacked the rest of the camp, killing about 100 Cheyenne, only 11 of them warriors. They took 53 women and children as hostages. These Cheyenne were the very people who had survived the earlier massacre at Sand Creek. Now they endured yet another massacre, as Custer and his troops shot at them, slaughtered hundreds of horses, and burned the village.

Afterward, Custer and his military superiors called the "battle" of Washita a great victory. For Black Kettle's people, it was a ghastly betrayal. Ironically, in 1876, it was Cheyenne who finally

Dull Knife (Tah-me-la-pash-me), the Northern Cheyenne chief who led his tribe at the Battle of Little Bighorn in 1876. (National Archives #96)

killed the long-time enemy of the Plains Indians, General George Custer, at the Battle of Little Bighorn.

Black Kettle was revered as a martyr of his people and of all Plains Indians who had pledged themselves to peace. The beloved and ever hopeful chief had waged a long, frustrating struggle to reach a clear agreement with the U.S. government. He had asked only that he and his band, who had never harmed any white person, could live on part of their land in peace.

OURAY

◆ ◆ ◆

The Changing Frontier

A group of nine Ute leaders arrived by train in Washington, D.C. one summer day in 1872. For years, these men had struggled to keep gold miners and settlers away from their lands in the present-day states of Utah and Colorado. A chief named Ouray was the principal spokesman as the group met with President Ulysses S. Grant in the White House. Ouray protested that whites were now taking lands the government had agreed belonged to his people. How many times, he asked Grant, were the Ute to be deprived of their territory and told to move onto smaller, less desirable land?

News accounts of Ouray's visit praised his speaking skills and dignified manner. During that week, one American official alleged that the Ute were lazy. Annoyed, Ouray retorted, "We work as hard as you do. Did you ever try skinning a buffalo?" Here was yet another example of the misunderstanding and anti-Indian prejudice that hurt relations between whites and Native Americans. Ouray spent most of his life expressing the concerns of his people and working for peace and justice during the onslaught of white settlement that took place in the West during the late 1800s.

◆ ◆ ◆

Ouray ("the arrow") was born about 1820 in present-day Taos, New Mexico, of a Jicarilla-Apache father and a mother who belonged to the Tabeguache (later called Uncompahgre) Ute. His

Ouray, the Arrow, leader of the Southern Ute. The Ouray Reservation of eastern Utah was named for the chief. (National Archives #112)

father was the chief of their band. As a boy, Ouray often worked for Mexican sheepherders who lived in the Southwest. A bright child, he learned to speak fluent Spanish, English, and several Indian dialects.

Ouray's own Ute language sprang from the Uto-Aztecan roots, as did those of the Bannock and Shoshone, who also lived in the Great Basin region. Basin Indians struggled to get enough food. Their dry desert surroundings provided little fish or game, so they hunted smaller animals, such as rabbits and squirrels, when they could find them. They gathered edible nuts, seeds, fruits, and grasses that grew wild in their region.

Through their contact with Spanish settlers in the Southwest, Southern Ute obtained horses and other goods, such as metal tools. With horses, the Ute could travel farther and hunt buffalo on the Plains. As a young man, Ouray was regarded as a brave warrior in battles against traditional Ute enemies, including the Sioux and Kiowa. Sometimes, the Southern Ute fought as allies of Spanish settlers against other European groups.

Not much is known about Ouray's activities until he was about 39 years old, at which time his first wife died. He also experienced deep sorrow when his only son was abducted by Sioux warriors during a raid on a Ute hunting camp. Ouray married again, this time to a Tabeguache woman named Chipeta. A year later, in 1860, his father died, and Ouray became chief of his band.

Ouray's talent for languages impressed white officials in the region. In 1863 he demonstrated his expertise in speaking and bargaining during treaty talks with the federal government at Conejos, Colorado. When the document was completed, he signed his name as "U-ray, the Arrow." After the meeting, he was offered a job as an official government interpreter. At a ceremony in Washington, D.C., Ouray received his title, along with medals and an annual wage of $1,000.

The mid-to-late 1800s were a time when western Native Americans were being told they must leave their ancestral lands and move onto smaller, limited areas called reservations. The Ute gave up lands east of the Continental Divide. In 1867 Ouray helped Christopher "Kit" Carson suppress a Ute uprising led by Chief Kaniatse.

Carson, who had served in the Union Army during the Civil War, had become a military officer. He was already famous as one of the legendary "mountain men." During the 1820s, the teenage Carson had come west to become a fur trapper in Taos, New Mexico, where Ouray was born. He and other mountain men trapped beavers and explored remote parts of the continent, showing other people what kinds of lands could be found there. When the fur trade dwindled in the 1840s, Carson turned to hunting and guiding settlers through the wilderness. Later he was appointed an Indian agent by the Bureau of Indian Affairs.

As settlers flowed into their territory, the Ute in Colorado, like other tribes, were being driven from their customary hunting lands. Miners in search of precious metals trespassed shamelessly on Ute lands during the 1860s. The wagon trains of settlers upset the game and buffalo in the area, which meant hunger and other problems for the Ute. The U.S. government hoped to confine them to a less desirable tract in Utah. In 1868 Ouray accompanied nine other chiefs and Agent Carson on his first diplomatic trip to Washington, where they spoke on behalf of seven Ute bands, including three northern ones (Grand River, Yampah, and Uintah) and three southern (Mouache, Capote, Wiminuche) and Ouray's, located in between. Their delegation succeeded in getting the Ute 16 million acres and two agencies to distribute needed goods and to help the Ute adjust to the reservation: Los Pinos for Southern Utes and Ouray's band and White River for those in the North.

When the government still failed to keep miners and settlers off Ute lands, Ouray and his wife Chipeta went on the 1872 trip to see President Grant. Despite Ouray's eloquent pleas and the efforts of his fellow leaders, the government called a new council at Los Pinos Indian Agency the next year. Federal officials asked the Ute to forfeit four million acres of their land in exchange for $25,000 a year in monetary payments. This was less land than the government had demanded the previous year, and Ouray concluded that these were the best terms he could obtain for his people. The agreement, known as the San Juan Cession, paid Ouray an annual pension of $1,000 as compensation for his help in reaching a peaceful settlement.

When the Los Pinos Indian agency moved to the Uncompahgre River in 1875, Ouray was given 400 acres and an adobe house near present-day Montrose, Colorado. The chief's friendship with whites and the favors he had received from them had offended some Ute through the years. Resentful enemies had tried to kill him on at least five occasions, but each time Ouray had saved himself by killing them first.

Colorado became a state in 1876, spurring profit-bent mining companies to launch a fresh effort to get rid of the three White River Ute groups. For several decades, these Indians had done

Ouray and eight other Ute leaders met with President Ulysses S. Grant (above) during an 1872 delegation to Washington, D.C. (Library of Congress #13018)

many favors for white settlers and the government. Some had worked as guides and interpreters, while Ute warriors had fought side by side with federal troops against other Indians, such as the Apache and Navajo. Nonetheless, "Utes must go!" became a popular political slogan in Colorado during the late 1870s.

Matters worsened in 1878 after a new Indian agent, Nathan Meeker, was appointed in the Northern Ute country at White River. He pushed the Ute to become farmers and tried to convert them to the Christian religion, but they rejected both of these ideas. Meeker asked federal troops to help him put down the dissidents, but the government did not act until 1879, when a series of fights, called the Ute War, broke out.

Ouray's brother-in-law Canalla led a group of warriors who were bitter that Ute grazing lands had been taken over for growing crops. They went to the White River agency, where fighting broke out between the Ute and Meeker's forces. The Indians killed Meeker and seven other whites at the agency, then held some women there as hostages, including Meeker's wife and daughter. When soldiers arrived, it looked as if violence would explode. Ouray was able to arrange for the hostages to be released unharmed. He pleaded the case of the Indian leaders as well, and they were not punished.

In a battle that September, Major Thomas T. Thornburgh led his regiment to a Ute camp. Chief Nicaagat, Chief Colorow, and about 100 warriors came forward to talk. But fighting broke out after Thornburgh ordered his men into battle formation and the Ute did the same. Thornburgh died during the shooting, and his troops retreated. A different commander led a new, week-long fight against the Ute. Again, Ouray was called to help negotiate peace.

By now, Chief Ouray was 59 years old and in poor health. Yet he undertook a third trip to Washington. White officials insisted that he sign a treaty that would assign the White River Ute to the Uintah Reservation in Utah where the Uncompahgre band was already living. Despite Ouray's loyalty and untiring efforts, all that remained of millions of acres of Ute homelands in Colorado was the Southern Ute Reservation in the southwestern corner of the state. There, the Nouache, Capote, and Wiminuche bands lived together. (Later, the Wiminuche would move to a tract in the western end, named Ute Mountain Reservation.)

On August 27, 1880, Ouray died of Bright's disease, a serious kidney ailment. He had just returned from Washington and was going to the new Southern Ute Agency at Ignacio. There, he was buried.

Sadly, Chipeta was not allowed to receive her husband's government annuity after he died. She lived in poverty on the reservation until her death in 1924, after which she was buried alongside Ouray, whose remains were moved to Montrose for reburial. Later, the Ute Reservation was named Uintah and Ouray Reservation in his honor, as was the town of Ouray, Colorado.

The career of Chief Ouray shows the difficult balancing act that many Indian leaders felt they had to do to enable their people to survive. Ouray was sometimes criticized by other Indians for being friendly with white settlers and the U.S. government. Yet his careful negotiations and peacemaking efforts enabled the Southern Ute to gain better treatment and a more desirable reservation than many other tribes received during the tumultuous 1800s. His work as a diplomatic spokesman also enlightened many non-Indians about the problems and mistreatment of Indians in the West. Seeing the eloquence and intelligence of Ouray and others, Americans realized that Indians were not ruthless savages but human beings who deserved fairer treatment. Although Ouray did not see the full results of his work during his lifetime, he, like other leaders, laid the groundwork for 20th-century efforts to redress years of injustice.

CROWFOOT

◆ ◆ ◆

Last Days of the Buffalo Hunt

In 1876, Crowfoot, leader of the powerful Blackfoot Confederacy, met with agents of the Canadian government at White River in what is now southern Alberta. Officials said the tribe must give its homelands over for white settlement. According to tribal history, one man showed Crowfoot a bundle of dollar bills and told him that the Blackfoot would receive money in exchange for their land. Crowfoot laid a handful of clay on the fire around which they had gathered, then asked the man to do the same with the money. The man refused. Crowfoot then told him, "Your money is not as good as our land. The wind will blow it away. The fire will burn it. Water will rot it. But nothing will destroy our land."

In spite of Crowfoot's best efforts to keep Blackfoot land, it was eventually lost to the government. Increasing white settlement and hunting also meant the end of the buffalo. With the demise of the buffalo came the tragic end of the Blackfoot's traditional way of life.

◆ ◆ ◆

Crowfoot was a Blood, born around 1821, at Blackfoot Crossing on the Bow River near present-day Alberta. His given name was Isapo or Sahpo Muxika. After his father died, his mother took him north to the Blackfoot lodge of her new husband. The Blackfoot included the Blood, the Piegan, and the Siska. They were a large group linked by their common language, religion, and customs.

The Blackfoot, a tribe belonging to the Algonquian language group, had come from lands in the north and east between Peace River and Saskatchewan, Canada. As they moved south to the area north of the Yellowstone River and east of the Rocky Mountains, they found more game, including antelope, elk, mountain sheep, moose, and deer. They were able to get horses, then guns, which allowed them to move down into the Plains. Theirs was a land of gorges and rugged mountains. Pine forests and winding rivers dotted the beautiful landscape.

After becoming skilled horsemen, the Blackfoot made buffalo meat the mainstay of their diet. The skins were used for clothing and shelter and other parts of the animal were made into tools. During these days of freedom and plenty, the tribe enjoyed a comfortable way of life, living in animal-skin lodges designed with smoke holes at the top. A lodge might be made up of 30 skins. When a camp moved, the lodges were torn down and transported by horses or travois (a sledlike vehicle consisting of two poles supporting a frame).

As a boy, Crowfoot, then called Nemorkian, spent much of his time with his half-brother Three Bulls. He learned to ride a horse and began to join the men for their early morning swims, even in cold weather. The Blackfoot claimed this practice helped them survive the long winters. After a meal that usually included boiled meat, the boys and young men rounded up their horses; then the older ones went out to hunt. Boys could spend the day engaged in hunting or games, or playing musical instruments and singing. Women tanned skins, butchered and dried meat, sewed clothing, and dyed moccasins the dark hue that had resulted in their tribe's unusual name. In the warm months, children gathered choke-cherries, wild seeds, berries, camas (an edible bulb that belongs to the lily family), bitterroots, and ducks' or small birds' eggs.

For feast days and other celebrations, Crowfoot combed his hair to make the customary side braids and knot on the forehead, often adding an owl feather. Young men also applied bright paint to their faces and sometimes to their bodies. Just about every Black-foot wore jewelry. Necklaces and earrings were made of shell, bone, teeth, and animal claws. Eagle feathers were coveted for headdresses, shields, and weapons. At night, Crowfoot and other young Blackfoot men might take part in social or war dances, donning an animal head mask for these occasions. Drums accompanied the stories and religious dances.

The Blackfoot were known as strong, swift-moving, fierce warriors. Their enemies were Flathead (now Confederated Salish-Kutenai), Kutenai, and Snake. Bravery was emphasized and boys were taught to excel in battle. "Better to die young as a brave warrior than to get old" was a common saying among this tribe. As a youth, Crowfoot became a great warrior, although it was his later peace efforts, as chief, that made him famous. He took part in the annual buffalo hunts—difficult maneuvers that took great skill to plan and execute successfully.

As Crowfoot reached his teenage years, the Blackfoot faced many new problems. White traders and trappers were swarming into the beaver-laden Missouri River region where his people lived. The Blackfoot snubbed the traders, so they built their posts in Crow country instead. Although they kept many whites away, the Blackfoot could not avoid the consequences of white settlement—one of the worst being an onslaught of diseases. Mandan Indians along the Missouri caught smallpox from trappers.

Smallpox almost wiped out the tribe, but a few survived and carried the disease to the Ree and the Arikara tribes. From there it struck the nearby Assiniboine and spread to Fort McKenzie, where some Blackfoot visitors caught it, taking the deadly virus back to their villages. Trading post–owner Alexander Culbertson described a Blackfoot camp that had been hit by smallpox: "Hundreds of decaying forms of human beings, horses, and dogs lay scattered about." Crowfoot was to witness four such smallpox epidemics. It is thought that his father, Chief Many Names, and most of the chief's children died of smallpox or tuberculosis (TB), a lung disease that was then incurable.

Crowfoot survived the 1837 epidemic and went on to excel as a warrior. Tall and slim, but muscular, he fought in 19 battles and was wounded six times. A priest once wrote that he "fought like a bear." His older brother had been honored with the name Crowfoot after fighting boldly against the Crow Indians. After this brother was killed by Snake Indians, Crowfoot was given his honored name for showing bravery in a revenge attack on the Snake. He earned a ceremonial robe of soft, white buffalo skins with bead designs of the sun and sacred symbols. Prized eagle feathers adorned his hat.

A rising leader, Crowfoot married a Blood woman his mother had chosen. They had a son and later adopted a son and daughter. At council meetings, people listened to Crowfoot's ideas with respect. He was also known for his generosity, often sharing his fine horses and taking time to teach young members of the tribe.

Unfortunately, the Blackfoot soon faced more problems. Cattle ranchers in the Southwest began sending their livestock north to graze in the Missouri-Yellowstone region, disrupting the food supply of the buffalo. As the buffalo population declined, some Blackfoot bands faced starvation. Helping his people survive thus became one of Crowfoot's biggest challenges.

By his thirties, he was a respected chief. His biographer, Ethel Brant Monture, says that Crowfoot "became convinced that to speak well for one's people was even better than to be a great warrior." As he realized that whites greatly outnumbered Indians and had superior weapons, Crowfoot concluded that it would be disastrous to fight them. Trying to calm angry warriors in the tribe, Crowfoot promoted the idea of peaceful coexistence with whites. He also worked to end warfare against other tribes, saying that it divided Native Americans and compounded their problems.

Crowfoot's influence kept his tribe neutral during an 1865 fight against Canadians called the Second Riel Rebellion, although his adopted son Poundmaker led a band of rebellious Cree Indians. While not taking part, Crowfoot's group helped escaping Cree find safe havens in Blackfoot tents. The next year, Crowfoot aided a white priest whom the Cree had captured. He was asked to mediate in disputes between whites and Indians in the region. In the early 1870s, he surpassed two other tribal chiefs to become the most influential Blackfoot chief.

Again, historical events were causing problems for his people. The Industrial Revolution had begun, and in 1871, a new process for tanning buffalo hides was developed. Now hides could be

A portrait of Crowfoot shows the Blackfoot leader looking thoughtful.
(National Archives of Canada/PA-134918)

made into a tough leather used for machine belts, much in demand as new factories sprang up in the eastern United States. At that point, there were still at least one million buffalo in northern Blackfoot country, but hunters began killing more than ever before. The bones of skinned buffalo lay scattered across the Plains.

As the buffalo herds declined, the Blackfoot lost their security and grew ever more dependent on whites for food and other necessities. In 1877 the Blackfoot were asked to meet with Canadian officials at the Bow River Council. At Blackfoot Crossing north of Fort Macleod, the Indians set up camp amid beautiful willows and wild roses. Crowfoot served as spokesman for the Blackfoot Confederacy—a heavy responsibility. He stayed alone in his tipi while thinking over the terms Canada had set forth.

On September 22, he signed Treaty No. 7. This meant the loss of 50,000 square acres of land lying west of the Cypress Hills, north of the international boundary, and east of the Rockies—what is now southern Alberta. Governor David Laird and Mountie commissioner James Macleod signed on behalf of the Dominion of Canada. Crowfoot, Old Sun, and Heavy Shield of the Blackfoot, and the other chiefs were offered medals and flags, but some refused.

Under this agreement, the Blackfoot became subjects of the British Empire under Queen Victoria. They kept the right to hunt in the land they had ceded in the treaty, but each tribe was assigned to a reservation. Families were given parcels of land within these reserves, and each person received a lump sum of $12 and an annual sum of $5. The Canadian government agreed to distribute $2,000 worth of ammunition and other goods: cattle, woolen blankets, flannel shirts, cloth, sewing thread, iron cookware, tin plates and cups, knives, farm tools, and seeds. Each chief was to receive an annual salary, ranging from $15 to $25.

Unfortunately, the Blackfoot suffered as a series of indifferent Indian agents came and left their region. They did not receive the goods and money they had been promised, and conflicts broke out. A missionary who traveled there said that incompetent agents had caused the problem. This missionary said that the Indians in the region were better behaved than the "ordinary white man."

During the late 1800s, the northern buffalo herds disappeared, causing starvation among many Plains Indians and the loss of their way of life. (©R. L. Kelly Pierre, S.D., South Dakota Historical Society)

Meanwhile, the demand for buffalo hides was taking its toll. At the 1877 Council of the North-West Territories, new laws took effect, banning the killing of buffalo less than two years old and shortening the killing season. But these laws were repealed the next year. By then, the herds were nearly gone. An outbreak of prairie fires occurred. U.S. troops set the fires to destroy the buffalo herds in order to punish rebellious Sioux led by Sitting Bull. The few herds that escaped to the south never returned after 1878.

By 1883 the northern buffalo herds had been destroyed. Later, the Blackfoot would call this the "starvation winter." Desperate, they ate gophers and other rodents, even horse meat. More than 600 Piegan died of hunger, tuberculosis, and other diseases. They needed help from whites merely to survive. The agencies distributed fat pork, beans, and hogs' heads. Some Indians became ill from this food. Others threw it out in frustration. As one Piegan said, "We didn't know how to cook these things." The government also urged the Indians to grow potatoes, turnips, and other crops. Crowfoot and other men disliked the idea of farming, and he maintained his horse herds instead. His people still trusted him and he remained head chief. He worked to improve their living conditions and successfully negotiated a trade-off of land when the Canadian Pacific Railroad crossed the Blackfoot reservation.

Hunger and deprivation led some Indians to rebel against the Canadian government in 1885. Once again, Crowfoot kept his people out of war. Now 64 years old, the chief increased his efforts to make peace among the Blood, Piegan, Sarci, Gros Ventre, and Assiniboine in Canada and Montana. He tried to mediate among those who were arguing among themselves. During his last years, Crowfoot traveled to camps and reservations, serving as a peacemaker.

As he aged, Crowfoot began experiencing poor health. It is thought that he suffered from tuberculosis. To his sorrow, his son also died at around this time. The tribe took care of their chief, and he continued to encourage them to adjust to their changing world as best they could.

The life of the Blackfoot had changed drastically during Crowfoot's lifetime. Once, the tribe had roamed a vast area on the northeastern Plains, secure in their way of life. Crowfoot lived to see the destruction of the buffalo and to guide his displaced people to their new, confined life on the reservation.

The disappearance of the buffalo hurt Crowfoot deeply. He had been born when these robust, brown-furred animals covered the Plains, providing a continual source of wealth and food for his people. When he died in April 1890, his last words were poignant and philosophical, and took note of the animal that had been the mainstay of the Plains Indians. He said, "What is life? It is the flash of a firefly in the night, it is the breath of a buffalo in the winter time. It is the little shadow which runs across the grass and loses itself in the sunset."

Crowfoot's insightful way with words was one of his most valuable contributions, not only as a Blackfoot leader but as a spokesperson for all Indians. Native Americans valued eloquence and wisdom far more than material goods, and orators were highly respected by their tribes. Crowfoot represented this value to the non-Indian world, gaining their respect, and, in some cases, also their compassion.

SPOTTED TAIL

◆ ◆ ◆

A Sioux Warrior Works
for Peace

In September 1855, Spotted Tail, a respected Brulé Sioux warrior, saw his people suffer the worst military defeat in their history. While fighting the Battle of Bluewater (in present-day Wyoming), 86 Sioux men died and Spotted Tail himself was badly wounded. Many of the tribe's horses were seized, and their camp was destroyed. After the battle, white officials cut off all trade and food distribution to the Sioux. They demanded that leading Sioux warriors in that region turn themselves in and go to prison.

Spotted Tail was one of three Brulé men who volunteered to surrender to soldiers at Fort Laramie. For this unselfish act he earned praise and gratitude from his people and the respect of the military officials at the fort. While Spotted Tail was serving a prison term at Fort Leavenworth, Kansas, he saw new and alarming things happening. Thousands of white settlers lived in the area, with hundreds more arriving each week. Shawnee, Delaware, and other Indians were living in white-style houses in areas called reservations, where they raised corn and even dressed like whites. According to biographer George E. Hyde, this experience made Spotted Tail aware of some unpleasant facts:

> He and his friends had been talking about the white people for the past twenty years, and now he suddenly realized how foolish most of that talk had been. The number and power of the whites were

frightening. Only a year ago he had been eager to fight the Americans. . . . When the Brulé prisoners reached Fort Leavenworth, the feeling that the Sioux could gain nothing by attempting to fight was overwhelming. This military post was something the Sioux had never dreamed could be possible. . . . This sudden realization of the number and strength of the Americans struck the Brulé captives a stunning blow.

Spotted Tail returned to his people with a changed outlook. He redirected his intellect and energy toward helping the Brulé find ways to live peacefully among the whites and trying to bring all Indians together. Charles Eastman, a Sioux who became a physician on South Dakota's Pine Ridge Reservation, reports that the chief once said, "Our cause is as a child's cause, in comparison with the power of the white man unless we can stop quarreling among ourselves and unite our energies for the common good."

◆ ◆ ◆

Spotted Tail (in Sioux *Sintegleska* or *Sinte Galeshka*) was born about 1823. His biographer, George E. Hyde, and other historians believe Spotted Tail was born in the White River country of present-day South Dakota or near Fort Laramie in Wyoming.

Centuries ago, the Brulé Sioux had come from Minnesota, and they were kin to the Santee Sioux, also from Minnesota. The name *Brulé* was given to them after the Sioux moved across the Missouri and split into seven different tribes, living mostly in South Dakota. French traders called this band *brulé* meaning "burnt," or "burnt thighs," because some tribal members had burn scars on their legs. They had been caught in a prairie fire, where some died and others escaped by running through the burning grass and leaping into a lake. After the Brulé and Teton Sioux came west, they sometimes went east each spring across the Missouri to trade with Santee. Their winter camp was at White Cliffs on the Cheyenne River near present-day Crawford, Nebraska.

Spotted Tail's people were originally friendly to the white trappers and traders who came to their camps and hunting grounds. They enjoyed a period of security and power between 1780 and

1820 when the deer, elk, and buffalo were plentiful. Brulé men also had a way of driving the antelope into traps by driving herds of them through gaps that led down the side of a cliff. With enough horses, food, and animal skins, they were able to survive and hold their own against enemies such as the Pawnee and Arikara. Sometimes, the Brulé's allies, the Miniconjou, camped with them.

Chief Makatozaza, or Clear Blue Earth, was leader during Spotted Tail's youth. A practical man, he helped his people organize hunts to make sure that every family obtained enough meat. During the early 1830s, Spotted Tail became a hunter and warrior. People later described Spotted Tail as having been a quiet, good-natured child who often played the role of leader or diplomat in games with other boys. Charles Eastman wrote that Spotted Tail had "his grandfather's wit and the wisdom of his grandmother." Eastman related an incident early in Spotted Tail's life in which two of his friends were arguing and then took out their knives. To divert them, Spotted Tail cried out, "The Shoshones are upon us! To arms! To arms!" The argument ended without bloodshed.

His grandson, Stephen Spotted Tail, later described how, as a young man, the chief received the "spotted tail" that was his trademark. Along with some friends, he was watching a white fur trapper skin a raccoon. The white man offered to give him the tail. It was customary for Sioux to wear talismans—objects or charms meant to bring luck—in battle, so Spotted Tail took the tail to use in a headdress for war and other occasions. He must have decided it brought good luck, for Spotted Tail wore the tail regularly and was soon being called by this new name.

By the mid-1830s, during Spotted Tail's adolescence, the buffalo herds were dwindling around the White River and Cheyenne River areas. Some Sioux groups were near the point of starvation. The Brulé were forced to move around more in order to find food. The Sioux also became closer to the Arapaho who lived on the Lower Platte. They hunted around the Kansas River and the North and South Platte but continued to have trouble finding enough food, especially during the bitter cold winters.

Spotted Tail became an expert hunter and a good marksman. During his late teens, he visited trading posts, where he studied the whites and accumulated knowledge about their habits and ideas. He liked to listen to discussions and meetings between the Sioux and whites. As he learned more English, Spotted Tail concluded that the whites were eager to acquire land and property.

Between 1835 and 1836, when Spotted Tail became a warrior, his tribe's main enemies were the fierce Pawnee who lived in the Lower Platte River region. George Bent, the half-Cheyenne son of trading post owner William Bent, wrote about an 1839 battle in which the Cheyenne and Sioux fought against Pawnee who had attacked and killed a large group led by a famous Cheyenne leader. (The Brulé had a long-standing feud with the Pawnee, which had intensified after 1838 when the Pawnee kidnapped a young Sioux girl and sacrificed her to their goddess.) Although only 16, Spotted Tail received the honor of being one of six men chosen as scouts. At a young age, he showed bravery and the ability to devise clever battle plans.

After proving himself as a hunter and warrior, Spotted Tail courted his first wife. He had fallen in love with Appearing Day, a tall, beautiful woman who had many other suitors. According to James McLaughlin, a former Sioux Indian agent, Spotted Tail and Appearing Day wanted to marry. But an older man, Chief Running Bear, had won her parents' approval. Spotted Tail was not put off. When Running Bear told him to stop pursuing Appearing Day, the two men began to fight with knives. When it was over, the chief was dead and Spotted Tail lay badly wounded. The girl's father was impressed with Spotted Tail's courage. After Appearing Day nursed him back to health, the two were married. Older tribe members told McLaughlin that the pair was very happy together.

Meanwhile, the Brulé encountered new problems. Their move to the Platte River region in the mid-1830s placed them right in the path of the main route white settlers were taking to Oregon. A trading post appeared on Laramie Fork in 1834, and trains of covered wagons streamed through the Platte Valley each year thereafter. The Sioux were surprised at their numbers, and white emigrants complained that Indians came up to their wagons, asking for food and taking rifles and horses. They asked the

Spotted Tail poses for a formal portrait with four of his sons.   (South Dakota State Historical Society)

government for more protection. Fort Laramie was strengthened and new posts opened.

Not much is known about Spotted Tail's activities during the period from 1841 to 1854. Some traders reported that in 1843, he was living among the Southern Oglala Sioux at Republican and Solomon Forks of the Kansas River. Around 1849, cholera and smallpox spread from white travelers to the Plains Indians, causing hundreds of deaths. The Indians asked for white medicine after their tribal healers could find no ways to treat or cure these unfamiliar diseases. Some Indians thought that evil white magic might be causing the sickness and death.

In 1851 Spotted Tail probably attended a council meeting at Fort Laramie. The Brulé camped there and received gifts and food from the white officials. At this time, Spotted Tail was not a chief, but rather a war leader. Three Brulé chiefs signed a treaty that said there should be peace and friendship among the people. The U.S. government pledged to distribute goods to each tribe every year for 50 years. Government officials hoped the Sioux would end their traditional hunting life-style and settle down on farms, as the settlers were doing, but the Plains Indians still rejected that kind of life.

Around this time, the Southern Brulé were camping on the Bluewater, a tributary of the northern Platte River. Spotted Tail and two other war leaders, Red Lead and Iron Shell, were urging their tribe to wage war on the whites. Spotted Tail's cousin, Brave Bear or Conquering Bear, was appointed chief. But he was killed by U.S. gunfire during a fight with whites. Feeling bitter, Spotted Tail joined an 1854 attack on U.S. soldiers.

Hostilities between the two groups continued, and in September 1855, white soldiers under General William S. Harney fought the Sioux at the Battle of Bluewater. Spotted Tail's wife and child were among the 70 women and children who were captured and taken to Fort Kearney to receive food and aid.

Spotted Tail and his comrades arrived at the fort chanting, riding fine horses, and dressed in ornate war costumes. One or more of Spotted Tail's wives, as well as a child or two, may have spent time with him during the two years he was held at the fort.

It was after his arrival at Fort Leavenworth, Kansas, in December 1855, that Spotted Tail was shocked at the numbers of white people and at the way local Indians were living. The officials at the fort soon learned they could trust Spotted Tail, so they allowed him a great deal of freedom. He learned much about white ways of life. Whites at the fort were friendly, and he became a popular

This photo, taken during the 1860s, shows Spotted Tail in white-style clothing with a kerchief around his neck. (South Dakota State Historical Society)

guest of the officers and their families. One of the officers had saved his baby during the Battle of Bluewater, and Spotted Tail expressed his gratitude.

Back home, he was applauded for his courage in having accepted imprisonment in order to restore his tribe's right to trade and receive goods. Spotted Tail was pardoned by the American president, James Buchanan. Now he prepared to lead his people, having learned things his fellow Indians were not aware of. Although he had not inherited the right to be chief, he was elected by his people.

When Sioux leaders began planning raids and attacks on American forts during the early 1860s, Spotted Tail was alone in questioning the wisdom of such fighting. Sitting Bull especially disagreed with him on this matter. Charles Eastman was told that Spotted Tail spoke these cautionary words during a speech at the great council on the Powder River just before the attack on Fort Phil Kearny:

> There is a time appointed to all things. Think for a moment how many multitudes of the animal tribes we ourselves have destroyed! Look upon the snow that appears to-day—to-morrow it is water. Listen to the dirge of the dry leaves, that were green and vigorous but a few moons before. We are a part of this life and it seems that our time is come. . . . Be not moved alone by heated arguments and thoughts of revenge. These are for the young. We are young no longer; let us think well, and give counsel as old men.

But the leaders decided to attack the fort anyway, and Spotted Tail joined them and was wounded during the fighting.

Wanting peace with whites, he joined the Southern Brulé who agreed with that policy. Spotted Tail's followers believed he had shown wise leadership during war and had a knowledge of whites. He was still leading battles against the Pawnee at this time.

As for his personal life, Spotted Tail may have had three or four wives by then. Among the Sioux, men married their wives' younger sisters. Chiefs had social obligations that required the giving of gifts—usually tanned and decorated animal hides that were made by women. So chiefs had other reasons besides custom to need more than one wife.

Between 1856 and 1864, Spotted Tail traveled perhaps thousands of miles a year on hunting trips and to conduct tribal business at various forts and camps. Often, he took a particular daughter of his, born in 1848, with him. She enjoyed seeing people she had met while staying with her father at Forts Leavenworth and Kearney.

Spotted Tail attended a commission held in 1867–68 to negotiate for his people and try to get decent terms if they were to be sent to reservations. He asked pointed questions of the white officials and agreed that his people would cooperate. Preferring to deal with Spotted Tail, General Crook tried to name him chief of all Sioux, but Spotted Tail refused to represent other bands, knowing it would cause animosity and add to his problems.

The war over the Bozeman Trail, leading into Montana, was being fought between Indians and whites during the period 1866–68. Like other trails, this one would make it easier for travelers to move west, disturbing the buffalo and other game in the process. Red Cloud led the Sioux in battles against the trail, while Spotted Tail urged them to come to terms with the whites. He did not want to give up the traditional Sioux life-style but had become convinced they had no other choice.

The U.S. government, for its part, did not recognize what it meant to the Sioux and many other Indians to give up the hunting and roaming way of life they had led for thousands of years. The idea of wounding Mother Earth with metal farm tools was also repulsive to these Indians. Spotted Tail was told that his people would be taken to a reservation by force, if necessary. While negotiating with white officials, he stressed that the Brulé wanted a say in where they would live and the right to hunt buffalo on Republican Fork. They were permitted to do this under an 1868 treaty. Along with some other Sioux chiefs, Spotted Tail signed the Fort Laramie Treaty that established the Great Sioux Reservation that year.

The Brulé were assigned to live at a new agency on Beaver Creek, in present-day Nebraska, called Fort Sheridan (later renamed Spotted Tail Agency). During this time, Spotted Tail was sometimes criticized by some of the Brulé for being too domineering and for becoming too proud because of the praise he received from white supporters. In 1870 Spotted Tail traveled to the eastern United States, where Quakers in Philadelphia praised him for his ongoing peace efforts. He met President Ulysses S. Grant in Washington, D.C. and spoke with the Seneca Ely Parker, who was commissioner of Indian Affairs. Spotted Tail went to Washington

Spotted Tail in 1872 during a trip to Washington, D.C. During several trips to the capital, the Brulé leader met President Grant and Seneca Ely Parker, then commissioner of Indian Affairs. (© Smithsonian Institution, neg. #43022)

several times more to negotiate better living conditions for his tribe.

Violence among Indians and gold miners led to the War for the Black Hills in South Dakota in 1876–77. Spotted Tail was appointed by the government to be chief of the Sioux at both agencies on the Sioux reservation. He helped to negotiate a settlement with Sioux militants in 1877. The U.S. government offered the Sioux $6 million for the Black Hills. After speaking with miners, Spotted Tail became convinced that the gold was worth much more than that. He made the government a counteroffer of $60 million, but they refused, staying with their original offer of $6 million.

There was more unrest for several years. The government relocated the Sioux agencies to South Dakota, renaming them Rosebud and Pine Ridge. Many Sioux were unhappy about the terms of the agreement that ended the conflict. They blamed Spotted Tail. A few men wanted to overthrow him and choose a new chief. A fellow Brulé, Crow Dog, supposedly told Spotted Tail he would "keep a bullet for him." Other people were angry at Spotted Tail when he eloped with a woman who was already married. She had left her husband's lodge to live in his.

Spotted Tail planned to offer the injured husband some goods for his wife, but before they worked out the problem Crow Dog intervened. He shot and killed Spotted Tail as he left his house at Rosebud on horseback on August 5, 1881.

Spotted Tail was deeply mourned by his family and friends. He was buried in his ornately beaded buckskin clothing at the agency. Later he was reburied in a cemetery north of Rosebud, and a white marble monument was placed over his grave.

Because of his reasons for killing Spotted Tail, Crow Dog was seen by his tribe as an executioner, not a murderer. Yet the state of South Dakota wanted him to be tried in their courts, not in the Sioux court. In 1883 the case became a major Indian rights matter. The U.S. Supreme Court pardoned Crow Dog in the case *Ex Parte Crow Dog*. The justices ruled that federal courts had no jurisdiction over crimes committed on reservation lands.

Two years later, Congress passed the Major Crimes Act, which reversed this ruling by saying that when an Indian committed a major crime (such as murder) against another Indian, he or she was subject to the laws of the state or territory in which the act was committed.

After Spotted Tail's death, no major new leaders stepped forward to unify the Brulé. White agents on the reservation were able

A portrait of Crow Dog, who killed Spotted Tail in 1881. A controversy over whether he should be tried by Indian or state courts eventually reached the U.S. Supreme Court and led Congress to pass the Major Crimes Act in 1885. (National Archives of Canada/C-34804)

to gain more control of the Sioux than they had had in his lifetime. Today, Spotted Tail is remembered in the Sioux Winter Count ceremony, with the words, "This year [1881] that brave and wonderful chief was killed by Crow Dog."

Like Washakie, Ouray, Crowfoot, and others, Spotted Tail was a distinguished warrior in his youth. Yet later his experiences convinced him that peaceful coexistence with white Americans was the best way for Indians to survive. Spirited and intelligent, with a charismatic personality, Spotted Tail impressed Indians and whites alike. He was able to gain the trust and affection of his people and to foresee how unity among Native Americans would improve their ability to gain their rights in the years to come.

WINEMA
(TOBEY RIDDLE)

◆ ◆ ◆

Brave Mediator in the Modoc War

The land of the Modoc, in present-day Oregon and California, is one of swift-running, rock-filled rivers and picturesque mountains. One summer day in the late 1830s, a Modoc girl named Nan-ook-too-wa was paddling a canoe on one of these rivers when a swift-moving current carried her into a rocky area. Her brother and sister and the other children in the canoe were terrified. But Nan-ook-too-wa stood up and bravely steered the canoe around the boulders, meanwhile trying to calm the other children in the boat. They managed to reach the level of the lake below the rapids safely, to the relief of Nan-ook-too-wa's father and other frightened onlookers.

For her courage, the Modoc named the girl Kaitchkona Winema, meaning "little woman-chief" or "woman of the brave heart." It was a name that she would earn many times over as she faced physical danger and the challenge of helping her people in the years ahead.

◆ ◆ ◆

Nan-ook-too-wa—"strange child"—was the name given to the woman born in 1836 who would later be called Winema or Tobey Riddle. Unlike most Indians, she had reddish-brown hair—a trait she inherited from her mother, who died shortly after she was born. Her father was Se-cot, and she had a cousin who later became a famous Modoc warrior known as Captain Jack.

Growing up in the Link River region of northern California, Nan-ook-too-wa enjoyed exploring Modoc country on her own. One of her favorite places was the hot springs, sacred to her people, on their land located about 20 miles north of the Oregon- California border.

The waters of Klamath Lake, which connects to the Pacific, form an inland sea here that contains numerous small islands. Picturesque mountains rise around the valleys and waters of Modoc country, and melting snow streams into Klamath Lake from the eastern Cascade range on the west. Besides the sacred springs, there are rocks with holes in them lying in one part of the river. Modoc legend says these are the footprints of God—Ka-moo-kum-chux.

After Winema showed her courage and received her special name, the Modoc chiefs and elders paid extra attention to her, sharing their tribal history and knowledge with her. Her father took her along on hunting trips and visits to white trading posts. Winema learned a great deal from her experiences and began to understand the English language.

Nonetheless, trouble was brewing as more white settlers crossed the country via the Oregon Trail to live in Oregon and California. The miners who had come west during the 1830s and 1840s were followed by thousands of other settlers. In his book *The Indian History of the Modoc War*, Winema's son Jeff C. Riddle later wrote that when the Modoc first saw covered wagons, sometime in 1848 or 1849, they "ran for the hills," thinking "God had sent Evil Spirits to punish them in some way." However, the Modoc eventually made friends with some of the settlers and treated them well. They enjoyed the bread, bacon, coffee, and tea the settlers shared with them.

Yet there was bloodshed in the region in 1853. A group of Pit River Indians (sometime enemy of the Modoc) attacked a wagon train near present-day Alturas, California, and killed some of the people. Survivors escaped to Yreka, where they told officials what had happened. A company of soldiers led by Captain Jim Crosby went out to find the Pit Indians, but was unsuccessful. All the Modoc they met were peaceful, but while they were asleep in Modoc country, a group of Pit River Indians attacked the troops.

After they escaped, the troops encountered some Modoc cooking a meal. Crosby ordered his men to fire on them. Only three of the 14 Modoc survived. When these people returned to the village and told others their story, it caused anger and fear. Some Modoc moved their camps, but Crosby's troops went on to kill more men, women, and children at the Hot Creek Modoc camp, even though these people approached them peacefully and there had been no declaration of war between the Modoc and the whites. Jeff Riddle wrote that Crosby's men were treated as heroes when they returned to Yreka carrying Indian scalps, but that "if the good citizens of Yreka had known the actual facts . . . they would have hooted Crosby and his men out of town. . . . It was such men as Crosby in the early days that caused the death of many good, innocent-hearted white people in the West."

About six months later, Modoc leaders attended a council at which they discussed their concerns. Captain Jack's father, who had called the meeting, warned, "I see that we cannot get along with the white people. They come along and kill my people for nothing. Not only my men, but they kill our wives and children." The chief and some other leaders concluded that they would all be killed unless they fought back. Winema's cousin Captain Jack, then only 14 years old, spoke up for peace, saying that there were too many white people to defeat and that the whites had confused the Modoc with the Pitt River group who attacked the wagon train. Jeff Riddle does not mention that his mother attended this meeting.

By 1853, Winema was considered old enough to marry and was being courted by a Modoc warrior named U-le-ta, who was in his twenties. Like other Link River Modoc, her father Se-Cot sometimes camped near the settlement of white miners who lived in Yreka, California. Winema often went with him, and during one visit she met Frank Riddle, who had been born in 1832 in Kentucky. Riddle visited the Indians as well and became familiar with

A portrait of Winema (Tobey Riddle) taken in 1873, at the end of the Modoc War. (©Smithsonian Institution, neg. #3051-B)

the vivacious, dark-eyed Winema. After Winema went home, her biographer Meacham says that the two missed each other. To be near him, Winema took her belongings from her father's home and went to stay with a cousin who had married a white man. Frank Riddle had been engaged to marry a girl from home, but he found himself falling in love with Winema. Winema told her cousin that she loved Frank.

During those years, it was the custom among the Modoc to choose mates for young people, but Winema asserted an independent spirit once again. She declared that she would wed Frank Riddle, despite the objections of her father and fellow Modoc. Winema and Riddle married in 1863 and lived in a cabin on his ranch. White settlers called her Tobey Riddle. With her quick intelligence, Winema learned to cook and keep house in a way that her neighbors called "first-rate."

Her tribe had rejected her for marrying Riddle, but they eventually grew to respect him. Riddle followed the Modoc custom of giving presents to his wife's people, bringing six horses to her father. Se-cot admired Riddle's marksmanship and entertaining stories. Frank Riddle accompanied the Modoc on hunting trips and other activities. He showed his bravery on one occasion by outrunning and outjumping a grizzly bear in the woods.

During these 1860s, some tribes in Southern Oregon were fighting among themselves. At times, members of feuding tribes came to trade in Yreka, where the Riddles lived. It was a major town in their region. Winema found that she had a knack for settling disputes among these people. Later the Modoc asked her and Frank Riddle to serve as interpreters and mediators between them and white settlers and officials. Her skills prevented violence on several occasions.

A treaty council was held between the Modoc and white officials at Yreka in 1864, shortly after Winema was married. She managed to persuade some reluctant Modoc leaders to attend. Frank Riddle and Winema helped the tribal leaders reach an agreement that they would make peace. By then, Meacham says, "she was universally known as 'the woman-chief' who could make peace . . . None knew her but to respect her." For several years after the Treaty of 1864 was signed, the Riddles enjoyed a calm life on their ranch, serving as interpreters and peacemakers when needed.

In 1869 whites began moving onto the lands where Winema's relatives, Captain Jack and his family, lived with their band near Tule Lake, separated from Klamath Lake by lava beds. These Modoc were near Lost River, which was rich in fish, duck, and

This 1873 group picture shows Winema, rear center, with her husband Frank Riddle at the right and an Indian agent on the left. Four Modoc women are seated in front. (Photo by Eadweard Muybridge, National Archives #72)

geese. Their land also held game animals and edible roots and bulbs. After fighting broke out between the Modoc and whites, these bands were forced to leave the land where they had lived for perhaps 9,000 years. Some fled to the mountains to avoid being arrested.

Government officials, led by Peace Commissioner Meacham, asked the Modoc to another conference in November 1869. Frank Riddle and Winema served as interpreters at the meeting. As leader of the Lost River band, Captain Jack, or Kintpuash or

Kei-in-te-poses ("Modoc chief of dark color"), had given up the idea of peace he had as a teenager. When the Modoc Peace Commission was called in 1865, he had refused to attend until Winema convinced the government agent to officially recognize Jack as a chief. At the 1869 meeting, the Modoc agreed to go to Klamath Indian Reservation in Oregon, where an agency had been established.

The officials agreed to protect the Modoc from the Klamath tribe if necessary. But at the reservation, there was trouble. In Jeff Riddle's account, the Klamath chiefs led raids on the Modoc camps, and one of them said, "This is my land. You have got no business to cut my trees down.... The grass, water, fish, fowl, deer, and everything belong to me." The Indian agent at Klamath told Captain Jack to move his people up Williamson River a few miles, but a few months later, they again had conflicts with the Klamath.

Frustrated when white officials did not help, Jack took his band back to Lost River. For a while, they lived in peace side by side with white settlers. Then in 1872, the Modoc were told that white troops would soon come after them. That November the secretary of war sent a telegram insisting that the Modoc be removed, by force if necessary. That marked the beginning of the Modoc War.

Winema was still working to make peace among whites and Indians. She also showed her courage during a visit to her tribe when Pit River Indians raided the camp and took horses, including the saddle horse her husband had given her. Winema helped to organize the Modoc warriors, leading them into a battle to recover their horses and defeat the aggressors. When she heard that troops were going to Lost River, she went to warn her cousin. Her son said that Winema urged Captain Jack not to resist the soldiers, but to go peacefully in order to avoid bloodshed. She rode about 75 miles that day to bring her message. She hoped that after the conflict ended, she could try to arrange for a new reservation for Jack's band along the Lost River. By now, Jack was said to have accused Winema of siding with the whites and being dead to her tribe.

Another fight broke out at Lost River when the soldiers came and told the Indians they must all give up their guns. Then the

Winema's cousin Captain Jack (Kintpuash), chief of the Modoc. Spurred on by members of his tribe and hostile whites, he led his people into the Modoc War. For shooting General Canby, he was hanged at Fort Klamath on October 3, 1873. (Photo by Louise Heller, National Archives #93)

settlers joined the soldiers in fighting the Indians. Captain Jack had always ordered his men never to hurt a white woman or child, but now the soldiers killed some Modoc women and children. Jack led the survivors to hide in the lava beds of Tule Lake, where men kept guard at all hours, alert for soldiers.

Many meetings followed as Frank Riddle and Winema carried messages back and forth between the Modoc rebels camped at the lava beds and the army officials. The fighting went on until February 1873, when Winema accompanied a group of white officials whom the Modoc trusted to hold talks at the lava beds.

A peace commission then met at a neutral campsite. The whites included General Edward Canby, Alfred Meacham, and Eleasar Thomas. Captain Jack was told to turn over a man named Hooker Jim so he could be prosecuted for killing some white ranchers, but he refused. The whites also would not promise Jack that his people could have a home in the Lost River area or the lava beds.

Winema was again asked to go back to the lava beds and persuade Captain Jack and his men to come, unarmed, to another peace meeting. As she was leaving with her son Jeff, born in 1863, a Modoc came up to her and told her that the Indian men planned to kill the whites at the meeting. Worried, Winema warned Meacham, who told General Canby, but Canby decided they should attend the meeting anyway. When the men gathered in early spring 1873, Captain Jack shot Canby with a revolver, and Bogus Charley, a Modoc warrior, cut his throat. Another Modoc warrior, Boston Charley, shot and killed Thomas.

When Chief Schonchin John shot at Meacham, Winema tried to disarm him, begging him not to kill Meacham. Meacham was shot seven times and fell down, although Winema threw herself in front of him to protect him. Boston Charley began to scalp Meacham, and she tried to pull his hands away. That effort failed, so Winema stood up and called out in Modoc, "Ut nah sholgars kep ko. Pelock genn nautt." ("Now the soldiers are coming; go quick all of you.")

After they left, Winema wrapped Meacham in her saddle blanket and left him there while she went on horseback to get help at a nearby camp. Halfway there, she met her husband and some soldiers, who went back for Meacham. Winema was determined to nurse him back to health. After two weeks in her care, he was able to return to his family in Salem, Oregon.

Once again, fighting raged between Captain Jack's group and the soldiers. When Jack was captured, he was executed. Meacham, who had once been his friend, was there at the time and promised Jack he would write his story. Meacham said that as Jack was being taken to prison, he said, "You talk for me. . . . The world won't hear me. I have no books or papers to talk for me. . . . You know all about it. You tell about . . . the soldiers stealing my horses and about General Canby moving his army near me while we were trying to make peace." Winema was also there and translated as the two men spoke.

Winema was much honored by the U.S. government. A parade in Washington, D.C. was held for her, and she met President Ulysses S. Grant. She, Frank, and Meacham toured the East from 1874 to 1881, visiting New York and other cities. Her son, Jefferson (Jeff), who had married the daughter of Modoc Chief Schonchin (a supporter of peace during the Modoc War who tried to keep the Treaty of 1864), traveled with her for a while. Scarfaced Charley and other Modoc also toured with her and told audiences about Indian concerns.

Winema lived her last years in Oregon, enjoying the companionship of her son, his five children, and her great-grandchildren. A pension of $25 a year was given to her in 1890, but she donated most of it to the Modoc people. She and Frank Riddle had a home at Yainax, Oregon, where he died in 1906 after a brief illness.

Her son later wrote *The Indian History of the Modoc War*, based on Winema's and other Indians' recollections. It was published in 1914. Winema died in 1932 on the Modoc reservation and was buried at the Modoc cemetery. There is a national forest named for her.

The Modoc, Winema's people, nearly died off after the war. Survivors of the Modoc War were sent to Oklahoma. In 1990 about 200 Modoc attended a ceremony to honor the tribe at the site of Lava Beds National Park near the Oregon border. This was the place at which Captain Jack had led 60 warriors to stave off 600 government soldiers in 1872.

Winema had dedicated her life to serving her people, while showing the courage and energy that had characterized her early years. Throughout her life, Winema showed an independent spirit, as well as the intelligence and compassion that enabled her to serve as a bridge between her people, the Modoc, and the white world that engulfed them.

ANNIE DODGE WAUNEKA

◆ ◆ ◆

Navajo Health Crusader

The hogan on the Navajo Reservation in Arizona was hot and stuffy, with the family living in tight quarters. Looking around, Annie Dodge Wauneka saw that these people did not have enough nourishing food. As was true of most hogans in the 1950s, there was no inside running water, making it difficult to keep everyone clean and to wash clothes and other household items. The dirt floor was an easy breeding ground for germs, and there were no windows to let in sunshine or fresh air.

Wauneka had come to visit a sick man who was coughing up blood. He had tuberculosis (TB)—an infectious lung disease that has existed throughout the world for centuries. Tuberculosis had killed many Navajo since the 1800s. During the 1950s, Wauneka studied TB and began helping her people to prevent and treat this disease. Now she spoke to the man and his wife, describing his disease in terms he could understand. Wauneka explained how the germs—which she translated as "bugs that eat the body"—could spread to other people when he coughed.

Her next goal was to persuade the man to accept medical help. If necessary, Wauneka would take him to the clinic herself, guiding him through the tests and procedures, then visiting him and his family to offer support. It was something she had done hundreds of times and would do hundreds of times more. As a leader in promoting the health, education, and well-being of the Navajo, Annie Dodge Wauneka was carrying on a proud tradition that had begun with her father, also an honored Navajo leader.

◆ ◆ ◆

Annie Dodge Wauneka was born on April 10, 1910, in the traditional Navajo hogan of her mother in what is now Old Sawmill, Arizona. The Navajo are a well-organized tribe that now number more than 130,000 people, making them the largest group of Indians in America. But in the decades before Annie was born, they endured terrible hardships.

Annie's father, Henry Chee Dodge, had lived through those turbulent times in the Southwest. As a small boy named Kiichii, he had been alone during the Civil War years. His father had died when he was only one, and his mother moved north, leaving him in the care of another Navajo family, who later moved away.

In previous centuries, the Navajo had been wanderers, or nomadic people, hunting, gathering, and raiding other tribes in the Southwest for what they needed. Gradually, they settled in more permanent villages, raising sheep, goats, cattle, and (after the 1500s) horses. From the Pueblo Indians in the region, they learned more about raising crops, weaving cloth from wool and other animal fibers, and making pottery. On the desert mesas, the Navajo developed a stable way of life amid their four sacred mountains—a place of vivid rock formations and dazzling sunsets. Water was scarce on the mesas, so the Navajo depended on streams supplied by the melting snow that cascaded down the mountains. Some of these peaks rose more than 10,000 feet above the desert. The Navajo located their communities near these small streams or underground springs so they would have water for drinking and for their crops and animals.

The Navajo's traditional ways of life changed after the 1600s when Spaniards and other white settlers moved into the Southwest. Throughout the early 1800s, Navajo and Apache warriors fought with U.S. Army troops. In 1860 the U.S. government decided to take control over the Navajo people and open their lands for settlement and the mining of gold and other valuable minerals. Two years later, white officials told the Navajo they must move to a military fort some 300 miles away.

Colonel Kit Carson led a regiment of soldiers and Indian enemies of the Navajo, including the Ute. The Navajo later said that during those dreadful days troops burned their cornfields and fruit orchards, took their animals, then pursued them, shooting and killing people. Historians are still debating Carson's role during this conflict, with some saying that he tried to help the Navajo and others saying he took part in the violence.

During that time, Annie's father, Kiichii, who was a young boy, met a somewhat older child, eight-year-old Shadi. She took him to the home she shared with her grandfather. Like other Navajo, they tried to flee from the soldiers but were overtaken. Some Navajo escaped capture but had to surrender when they faced the possibility of starving that winter.

The soldiers led about 8,000 Navajo prisoners on what was later called the Long Walk. People marched nearly 300 miles across mostly desert land to Fort Sumner on the Bosque Redondo Reservation in what is now New Mexico. Young and old, sick and well, even pregnant women, were told to keep pace with the group during this exhausting journey. Like the Cherokee and other tribes before and after, the Navajo were being removed from their homes by force.

During his four years as a captive at Fort Sumner, Annie's father, whom people began calling Chee, saw terrible suffering. Crops were so meager that many people died of hunger and malnutrition. Diseases spread rapidly among the weakened people, and an unusually high percentage of infants died. People lined up to receive unfamiliar foods, such as coffee, tea, and white bread, called rations, from government agents.

A bright young man, Chee was well-liked by both the Navajo and the military people. He learned to speak English so well that he was often asked to interpret for whites and Navajo. Along with the others, Chee was released in 1868. The government told the Navajo they could either move to Indian Territory (now Oklahoma) or return to a portion of their former homeland if they

Annie Wauneka's father, Henry Chee Dodge, was a respected tribal leader for many years. (Navajo Historic Preservation Dept.)

agreed to live peacefully inside a designated area. The Navajo signed a treaty, glad they could once again live near their sacred mountains and try to resume their old ways.

Chee moved with Shadi and her grandfather to a place north of Fort Defiance near the Chuska Mountains. There he tended a flock of sheep, for the government had given the Navajo small herds to help them get started on their own. At age 12, Chee met one of his aunts, and she told him that his father had been a Mexican who also worked as an interpreter. Chee's name was actually Henry Dodge, so he became known as Henry Chee Dodge.

Working in a supply room at the fort and as an army interpreter, Dodge earned $5 a month. Years of hard work and thrift enabled Henry Chee Dodge to accumulate land and livestock. By age 30, he was a wealthy man. He owned a ranch and acres of land in Arizona, with horses, sheep, and cattle herds. A prominent architect designed a spacious home for him at Sonsela Mountain near the Navajo capitol of Window Rock, Arizona. It was beautifully furnished and decorated with Navajo rugs and artwork.

Chee Dodge met and married Shadi's daughter, Nanabah. In keeping with Navajo custom, he also married her younger sister. Within a few years, he had three children—Mary, Tom, and Ben. Nanabah had a cousin who needed a husband, so it was arranged that Chee would take K'eehabah as his wife as well. K'eehabah gave birth to a daughter whom she and Chee named Annie.

When Annie was one, she left her mother's hogan for her father's Sonsela Butte home. It was located in a picturesque setting of red-toned rocks, rugged cliffs, sagebrush, and pines. There was grass and water for the large herds of sheep and cattle her father raised. Chee Dodge's wealth brought his family many privileges and comforts, such as access to health care and good schools.

Annie saw that her father valued his Indian heritage and that people treated him with great respect. This was also a great tribute to Dodge, for the Navajo do not glorify wealth or material possessions. They admire personal qualities, such as service to others. Chee contributed his time and money to his people and was often called upon to make key decisions or to negotiate with tribal leaders and white officials.

By age five, Annie was given a big responsibility of her own: She was in charge of tending a flock of sheep. After a traditional breakfast, perhaps lamb stew and fry bread (a puffy pan-fried bread made with corn flour), Annie would guide her flock up the grassy foothills of the ranch. Some of the sheep she watched were hers, gifts from her father. As the day went on, Annie took care that the sheep had enough water and did not eat more grass than was good for them. She made sure they did not accidentally eat the poisonous plants that also grew on the hills. It was a big job for a young child, but Annie showed she could do it.

Soon Annie began attending the government school at Fort Defiance. During the years she was seven and eight, a severe influenza epidemic spread all over North America and the rest of the world, hitting the Navajo reservation hard. Thousands of Navajo died during this epidemic, as there were no medicines that could kill this virus.

Annie was lucky to get only a mild case of the flu, from which she recovered completely. Since she was immune—resistant—to another attack, she helped the school nurse care for the sick children at school. Some were too weak to eat, and Annie fed them soup, spoonful by spoonful. But so many died that there were not enough wooden coffins or people to help with their burials. A mass grave was dug near the school for these young victims.

During this crisis, Annie developed a strong interest in helping others and in the area of health care. The epidemic over, she returned to her studies, earning such good grades that her father enrolled her at the Albuquerque Indian School where her half-sister Mary was studying. There Annie learned English and met Pueblo Indians from other tribes. She also became friends with a fellow student named George Wauneka.

In 1923 the Navajo Tribal Council held its first meeting and elected Chee Dodge as tribal chairman. As a teenager, Annie grew quite familiar with tribal politics. Her father noticed Annie's intelligence and good judgment and often took his tall (nearly six-foot) daughter with him to tribal meetings or to visit Navajo homes. Her father's approval must have meant a lot to Annie, for she had not always felt as accepted in the family as her half-sister and half-brother. Her mother, being the third wife, did not have the same household role as did Mary's mother, Nanabah, Chee's first wife.

While visiting Navajo homes with her father, Annie became concerned about the poverty and other problems she witnessed. Although Chee's chairmanship ended in 1928, he continued to be a major tribal leader. Important visitors still visited Dodge, and the family discussed current events, politics, and tribal issues.

That same year, Annie completed 11th grade and stopped attending the Albuquerque school. She returned home and told her father that she and George Wauneka wished to marry. Navajo parents typically arranged marriages for their children, but Chee Dodge and Nanabah approved of George and his family and thought the match was a good one.

The Waunekas were married in October 1929. In traditional Navajo style, Annie Dodge wore a festive, printed calico skirt and long velveteen overblouse, adorned with fine silver and turquoise jewelry from the family's collection. Her black hair was pulled back from her face and twisted into a bun behind her neck.

The newlyweds spent two years at Sonsela Butte; then Chee Dodge asked them to manage his Tanner Springs ranch, where they would be in charge of large herds of cattle, sheep, and horses. Both Chee and his wife sent their herds to Tanner Springs each winter because there was a good supply of water and grass there. Annie Wauneka proved to be both a good manager and a skilled homemaker. The family grew as children came along: Georgia Ann in 1931, Henry in 1933, Irma in 1935, Franklin in 1945, Lorencita in 1947, and Sallie in 1950. Their home was modern by Navajo standards, with running water and electricity. A school and a trading post were located near the ranch.

While busy rearing her children and working on the ranch, Wauneka continued to help her father as he attended meetings and visited needy families. Until he died in 1947, Chee Dodge helped his people to improve their economy and educational system. His business skills helped the Navajo to make the most of the income they received for oil and uranium deposits; his practical ideas helped them to make hard decisions through the years.

Meanwhile, Annie Wauneka was becoming an esteemed leader in her own right. In 1951 she became the first woman ever elected to the Navajo Tribal Council. At the time, there was much disagreement between the more modern and traditional factions of the tribe about whether a woman should serve on the council. But Wauneka did such a good job, she was reelected in 1954 and 1959.

A recent photo of Annie Dodge Wauneka shows her wearing a Navajo necklace from her family's collection. (Navajo Historic Preservation Dept.)

When Wauneka first joined the council, she was assigned to head the Health Committee. Although this was a difficult job that required her to be exposed to illnesses, Wauneka wanted to tackle it. Tuberculosis, a serious lung disease, was one of her greatest challenges. The ceremonies and traditional plant medicines used by Navajo healers did not quell the disease. Many people were dying, and those who had TB spread germs when they coughed or were in close contact with others who breathed the same air.

Wauneka spent three months studying different aspects of the disease with the U.S. Public Health Service. She visited laboratories, examined chest X rays, and read about the antibiotics and other treatments that white medical doctors used. When sharing this knowledge with her people, Wauneka was careful to explain things in terms they could understand. She did not wish to belittle the efforts of tribal medicine men, so she explained that tuberculosis was a powerful disease that had struck people everywhere in the world. Therefore, the medicine men might not be able to cure it all alone. By joining forces with white medicine, they could work to help TB victims, Wauneka said. By speaking clearly and carefully, she convinced people to get help.

Besides attending meetings and visiting patients, Wauneka wrote a glossary of medical terms in English and Navajo. Patiently, she taught people about sanitation and showed them ways to keep diseases from spreading. The Public Health Service agreed to build new hospitals and clinics throughout the reservation. Because of Wauneka, thousands of people had diagnostic chest X rays and entered the hospital for treatment, a process that saved many lives. She also worked to establish eye, ear, and dental care programs on the reservation. Preventing illness, as well as treating existing problems, was vital, she believed.

Toward that end, Wauneka planned innovative ways to get health information to people. She knew that many Navajo enjoyed listening to their radios, so she developed a program that was broadcast every Sunday. Speaking in Navajo, she discussed pregnancy, baby care, childhood immunizations, healthy eating, food preparation, and clean water, among other things. Wauneka also spearheaded two movies on health and sanitation that were used in schools and at public gatherings. To increase her knowledge, she read widely about health and other issues, a lifelong habit.

A practical person, Wauneka knew that talk alone was not enough. She urged Navajo leaders to set aside funds so that people could install glass windows in their hogans and replace dirt floors with wooden ones. As she told people about the benefits of fresh

air and cleanliness, they began to carry out these changes. Gradually, more people abandoned the traditional hogans and began
building wooden or cinderblock homes that sometimes kept the
traditional rounded shape. More water and sewer lines were built
throughout the reservation to improve the Navajo's access to
water and plumbing.

Often, Wauneka has faced and overcome tremendous opposi-
tion to her proposed changes. She has said that the foundation of
her success is her effort to gain people's trust. She also respects
their opinions and decisions. After explaining their choices,
Wauneka says, "I let them make their own decisions on what to
do." Their esteem for her was clear when Wauneka received the
Indian Council Fire Medal in 1959.

Wauneka's ongoing work has brought her national attention.
She was invited to appear on a television news program called
"Twentieth Century," with well-known journalist Walter Cronk-
ite. In 1963 she became the first Indian to receive the Presidential
Medal of Freedom. President John F. Kennedy had conferred the
award but was killed before he could present it. That December,
President Lyndon Johnson gave Annie Wauneka what is called the
highest civilian honor an American can receive.

Besides these awards, Wauneka has been named Arizona's
Woman of the Year and was one of several prominent women to
receive Woman of the Year awards in 1976 from the *Ladies' Home
Journal* magazine. Although she left high school after the 11th
grade, Wauneka has continued to learn throughout her life. Her
achievements and knowledge have been recognized with several
honorary degrees, including an honorary doctor of humanities
degree from the University of Albuquerque in 1972. She is an
honorary lifetime member of Society for Public Health. Two of her
daughters followed their mother's example and joined the Public
Health Service.

Wauneka has a long list of accomplishments, including her
work for the Navajo Area health board, Project Hope, the Navajo
Nation School Board Association, and the Navajo Tribal Unity
Authority. Her concern about health has also led to her involvement in the National Public Health Education Association, the

American Public Health Association, and the National Tuberculosis Association (now the American Lung Association). She has worked closely with Navajo Girl Scout programs and encouraged these young women to help with health care on the reservation.

As tuberculosis declined among the Navajo, Wauneka turned her attention to other health problems. Her work in sanitation and for safer food and water led to reduced rates of food poisoning and diseases of the stomach and intestinal tract. Since the 1970s, she has worked to curb drug abuse, as well as the more widespread problem of alcohol, which Wauneka once called "the number one killer on the reservation today."

"Work for the benefit of our people," Chee Dodge had told his children before he died. Wauneka has done just that since her early years. She has faced problems that caused others to give up and that took determined work to resolve. But Wauneka believes one must always keep trying. She once said, "One failure—or even a half-dozen failures—should never be the end of trying. I must always try and try again, and I will continue to try as long as there is breath to do so."

A respected tribal leader in her eighties, Annie Dodge Wauneka still works for causes she has promoted for decades. Mother, grandmother, businesswoman, political leader, educator, health advocate—hers has been a rich, full life. She continues to lecture, and she leads community action projects with the National Health Service.

While advocating changes to improve health, education, and employment, Wauneka speaks highly of Navajo language and beliefs and takes part in the traditional ceremonies. Like Winema of the Modoc and newer leaders, such as the Cherokee Wilma Mankiller, she has blended new ways with old, using her knowledge to help her people. As the citation that accompanied her Presidential Medal of Freedom read, "she has helped dramatically to lessen the menace of disease among her people and to improve their way of life."

ADA DEER

◆ ◆ ◆

A Menominee Leader Heads for Washington

In her 1970 autobiography, Ada Deer said, "When people tell me, 'No, you can't,' I am determined to show them that 'I most certainly can.' That includes speaking up and speaking out." As a social worker, tribal advocate, professor, and public servant, Ada Deer has worked hard to improve the lives of Indians and other Americans. She has overcome discrimination and other obstacles to pursue her education and her many-faceted career. In 1993 Deer took a new job in Washington, D.C., where she has fresh opportunities to use the vision and practical skills that have characterized her life. Praising these qualities and her rich contributions to her tribe, Menominee tribal chairman Glen T. Miller once called Ada Deer "a dreamer with power."

◆ ◆ ◆

Ada Elizabeth Deer was born on August 7, 1935, in a hospital on the Menominee Reservation in Wisconsin. The family included nine children, four of whom died in infancy. Ada's father, Joseph Deer, was a full-blood Menominee who had grown up on the reservation and had experienced many problems, including poverty, during his youth. In contrast, her mother, Constance Wood Deer, had grown up in a socially prominent white Philadelphia family. Her minister father received a generous income from stock in his family's business, and the Woods lived in a large, elegant home staffed by servants. However, Constance wanted a different kind of life. Her family disapproved when she chose a nursing career over marriage, then went to work for the Bureau of Indian Affairs. While working on the Menominee Reservation, she met and married Joseph Deer.

From ages one to six, Ada lived with her family in a cabin on Wolf River near Keshena, Wisconsin. There was no indoor running water or electricity, and the children helped to carry water and chop wood, among other chores. As Ada grew older, she helped to care for her younger brother and sister. She learned to appreciate the natural beauty of the rural area, with its animals, quiet forests, and clean water for swimming.

When she was five, Ada first encountered prejudice against Indians. Although she had never met her Wood relatives, one day her mother's father and twin sister came to her family's cabin, trying to persuade Constance to return to her former home. Ada was deeply hurt by the unkind way they rebuffed her and the other children. She later said, "I began to discover that I was different. And for the first time, I sensed that I could be hated and called names because of it."

Although still very young, Ada also became aware of the difficulties her people faced on the reservation. One of these was using too much alcohol, something that caused family conflict and health problems. In her autobiography, she wrote, "Many Indians drink too much. Life on the reservation has a way of draining ambition from all but the most determined Indians. And liquor has a way of blurring the bleak reality of a dusty life that seems without hope."

When the United States entered World War II in 1941, Ada was six years old. The family decided to move to Milwaukee so Joseph Deer could get a factory job, which paid higher wages than he could earn on the reservation.

Living as the only Indians in their neighborhood on the city's South Side, the Deers encountered some hostility. A neighbor used to tell the children to go away, screaming, "Go back where you came from." Ada said that as she grew older, she realized how ridiculous that remark was, since her father's family had lived in America for thousands of years and the Wood family had come more than 300 years before. But to a young child, this was a painful lesson in how cruel people could be, judging others they didn't even know because of their race or color. Children also teased the Deers and called them "dirty Indians." Ada hated being called a "squaw," an insulting name for Indian women.

When Ada started school, she was eager to learn but felt shy about speaking up in class. Her mother told her she must learn to express herself so that the teacher would know she had learned her assignments. Ada also was curious about her Menominee heritage and asked her father questions about their culture and language. She was surprised that he showed no interest in sharing these things. Her mother explained that as a child, Joseph Deer had been sent to a federal boarding school, where he had been taught to reject his native ways and adopt the white language and customs. (Later, Ada's father showed a renewed interest in Menominee ways, mastering the language superbly.)

When Ada was 10, the family moved back to Keshena. Ada's brother had a health problem that required goat's milk and they could not get it in Milwaukee. Ada changed to a new public school 10 miles away. During the winter, she and her mother rose before the sun to clear the roadway so that the school bus could come through. As in Milwaukee, Ada was a good student but was left out of social activities and games at recess. In eighth grade, when she attended school dances, the white girls made fun of her clothes.

Ada tried not to mind, and focused on doing her best in school. Her family's support and encouragement helped her to realize she was as good as anyone else. Teachers who recognized Ada's potential also encouraged her to work hard and aim for college. In her senior year of high school, Ada edited the school annual and won a speaking contest. She was appointed to the Governor's Commission on Human Rights. A different kind of recognition came her way when Constance Deer urged her daughter to enter a contest to find the "six most beautiful Indian girls in America." Ada was selected along with five others and won an expenses-paid week in Hollywood, California, the summer after she graduated from high school. She and the others were interviewed and attended dinners and parties in their honor. They also appeared in a western movie, *The Battle of Rogue River*. Speaking ruefully of the film, Ada later said, "The Indians, of course, were the bad guys."

Ada graduated from high school in 1953, a year of historic importance for the Menominee tribe. Congress was finishing work on the Menominee Termination Act of 1953. The Bureau of Indian Affairs had decided that Indians should move away from the idea of reservations and tribal status and stop receiving government support and protection. Termination was meant to end group ownership of land and tax exemptions and to encourage Native Americans to become assimilated into the general population.

The Menominee of Wisconsin then numbered about 6,000 people. Before whites settled their region in the 1700s, they had occupied some 9.5 million acres. Food was plentiful, making it possible for people to live in organized communities of semipermanent villages. They had hunted deer, elk, and smaller game and gathered wild fruits, roots, and wild rice (*omehnomehneuw*). The rivers held trout, sturgeon, and other fish, and some Menominee also raised crops.

At the height of the fur trade (1667–1838), the Menominee moved about more often. They traded furs for tools, cloth, blankets, and rifles, but did not abandon their traditional language, spiritual beliefs, or crafts. During the 1800s, their lands were reduced along with those of other tribes. The 1854 Wolf River Treaty guaranteed them 250,000 acres of their land forever, but the acreage was reduced in the following years. The Menominee developed a timber business, which gave them more income than many tribes had. For that and other reasons, they were the first to be "terminated" in the 1950s. When that policy went into effect, the consequences for the Menominee were disastrous.

As these events were unfolding, Ada Deer was entering the University of Wisconsin at Madison. She had desperately wanted to attend college, despite her family's poverty, and her academic record and test scores enabled her to win the Menominee Tribal Scholarship. Deer was still on the Youth Advisory Board of the Governor's Commission on Human Rights, and she met a much more diverse group of people in college—blacks, Hispanics, Asian Americans. Some of the community projects planned by the group won a *Parents* Magazine Youth Achievement Award. She also represented the group by speaking at high schools throughout the country.

A social work major, Deer made the most of her opportunities at the university and became the first Menominee to graduate from that school. She was accepted into graduate school at Columbia University, in New York City. There, she would become the first Native American to receive a master's degree from the Columbia School of Social Work, as well as the first of her tribe to earn a master's degree. At Columbia, Deer studied community organization and group social work. One of her field assignments was at the famous Henry Street Settlement, where she helped people find community resources to get housing, financial aid, health care, and other things they needed. A fellowship helped pay expenses.

In between her two years of graduate school, Deer spent two years out of school as a social worker in the poor Bedford-Stuyvesant area of the city. She returned to school in 1959 feeling more mature and experienced. Deer chose to write her thesis about community organization on New York's Lower East Side.

After graduation, Deer found a job working with Indians at the Waite Neighborhood House in Minneapolis, Minnesota. There, she helped Native Americans who faced urban problems, something she understood keenly from her own experience. This was also the time that the official termination of the Menominee was taking place. Their community property was declared private property, and much of it was sold without planning. Without adequate preparation, the Menominee were on their own.

In 1962 Deer met with Dr. Philleo Nash, the commissioner of the Bureau of Indian Affairs, in Washington, D.C. She expressed her concerns about the Menominee, later saying, "I felt that the BIA should have prepared the Menominee for termination by helping them set up an effective local government."

Nash was so impressed with Deer that he offered her a position with the bureau in 1964. She agreed to work as a community services coordinator in Minnesota. Before she began her new job,

she was asked by Nash to spend several months traveling throughout the United States and learning as much as she could about
Indian affairs. She learned a great deal from the experience, and
was eager to put her insights into practice. But when she returned
to Minnesota, her job had been abolished, and the new area
director told her she would be working as an employment counselor. Frustrated by her lack of influence, Deer left the bureau after
spending three years there.

Afterward, she spent a year with the University of Minnesota
Indian Project, then became a counselor at an inner-city school that
served minorities, including some Indians. Again, Deer felt she
was struggling against "a brick wall." She saw students with many
problems at home and at school that were not being properly
addressed. About half the students could not read.

Deer next worked at the Stevens Point campus of the University
of Wisconsin, in an Upward Bound project to help minority students prepare for higher education. This was an exciting way to
make a difference. As Deer later said, "I had long ago realized that
many Indian kids have great potential. However, they usually
don't know it. . . . Often the schools are to blame for not knowing
how to work with Indians but the kids get down on themselves."
At the university program, students would spend six weeks during the summer in a special series of courses that covered such
subjects as math, reading, art, drama, and Indian history.

By the late 1960s, when Deer was starting law school in Minnesota, the Menominee faced severe problems. As a result of termination, poverty and unemployment were soaring, and people
lacked decent health care. Many acres of land had been sold. Deer
decided not to pursue her law degree and went home to help lead
a restoration movement that aimed to revoke termination. The
Menominee protested land sales and staged a 200-mile march to
Madison, the capitol of Wisconsin, to bring attention to their
plight. Deer's friend Lucille EchoHawk later said, "she led through
consensus, involving thousands of Menominee people and drawing out the best in them. . . . By 1972, the Menominee Restoration
Act was introduced in the U.S. Congress and with Ada leading the
lobbying effort, it was signed into law the following year." Deer

A recent portrait of Ada Deer. (Courtesy of Ada Deer, photo by David Loeb)

later called the act "a vivid reminder of how great government can be when it is large enough to admit and rectify its mistakes."

The tribe had also waged a court battle that reached the U. S. Supreme Court as *Menominee Tribe v. United States*. The Court ruled that termination had not affected their right to hunt and fish on their former reservation lands. This ruling helped set the stage for the reversal of the Menominee termination. Afterward, other tribes were heartened to followed this example and have their own status and lands restored.

In addition to her job and her two-year lobbying effort in Washington for the restoration movement, Deer was busy with many other activities. She joined the national board of the Girl Scouts, U.S.A. after she became convinced that the organization wanted to help Native American girls and other minorities. From 1967–68, Deer served with the Joint Commission on the Mental Health of Children and attended the White House Conference on Children and Youth, and served with the Urban Indian Task Force of the Department of Health, Education, and Welfare. In 1970 she also joined the Washington, D.C.–based Americans for Indian Opportunity, a group she would work with for the next 13 years.

The Menominee appointed Deer as chairperson of the Restoration Committee, a post she held from 1973–76. One of the committee's greatest tasks was to impress upon the federal and state governments the importance of preserving the forests on the Menominee lands. Within the tribe itself, some men had been skeptical about how effectively a woman could lead this kind of effort. Through persistence and skill, Deer and other Menominee women worked to overcome the same prejudices that Navajo Annie Wauneka and Cherokee Wilma Mankiller faced in becoming leaders.

Deer proved effective as a leader both in her tribe and in her profession. Her personal and work experiences gave her a deeper understanding of rural and urban poverty and of the problems people, especially minorities, faced in daily living. New learning and leadership opportunities came with Deer's growing reputation. She was selected as a fellow at the John F. Kennedy School of Government at Harvard in 1977–78. In 1978 and 1982, she decided to run for the Democratic nomination for state treasurer of Wisconsin, but was unsuccessful. Between 1978 and 1980, she served as the president of the Association of American Indians and Alaska Native Social Workers. (Ten years later, she would serve as president of the Wisconsin chapter of the National Association of Social Workers.)

Her work with other organizations revealed her concerns about unemployment, housing, education, human rights, and the welfare of children. Deer also became a lecturer in Native American affairs at the University of Wisconsin, where she had once been a student. There, she had the chance to share her vast experience and ideals with students.

In 1991 Ada Deer decided she could serve people in other ways by running for the U.S. Congress. She entered the race for representative of the Second Congressional District in Wisconsin. David Clarenback, whom Deer defeated in the primary to win the Democratic nomination, said the race was "vigorous and principled." He said, "She proved to everyone what I have known for years: She's a forceful advocate for the progressive causes we share. She's made a believer out of a lot of people."

Deer ran her campaign mostly with the help of dedicated volunteers and on a tight budget. Early on, she announced that she would not accept contributions from PACs (political action committees) so that she would not owe anything to special interest groups once she arrived in Washington. Many national figures, including the Reverend Jesse Jackson and feminist leader Gloria Steinem, came to Wisconsin to express their support for Deer. She received numerous newspaper endorsements, including one from the *The* [Milwaukee] *Daily Cardinal* that said, "Ada Deer has immersed her existence in the often impossible battles for social justice."

If elected, she would have been the first woman congressperson from Wisconsin and the first Native American woman ever elected to Congress. Deer campaigned vigorously, stressing her record as an activist and telling voters she would bring a fresh, independent perspective to Washington. At one point, campaigning in tennis shoes at Madison's farmer's market, she promised, "When I get to Washington, I will hit the ground running."

Ada Deer delivers a speech during her 1992 congressional campaign. One of her campaign slogans was "Nobody runs like Ada Deer." (Courtesy of Ada Deer, photo by David Loeb)

Deer's opponent, a well-liked, articulate former newscaster named Scott Klug who had just finished his first term in Congress, was reelected. Deer was naturally disappointed; yet the 1992 campaign had been a positive and thrilling experience, one that Deer said "made me feel my power." She described the joy she had felt standing beside candidate (now president) Bill Clinton and his running mate, Al Gore, as 30,000 people cheered them and their agenda for the nation: "Let me tell you, that's exciting."

Impressed with Deer and her achievements, the Clinton administration asked her to come to Washington. In 1993, she was appointed assistant secretary of Indian affairs in the Department of the Interior—the first woman to serve in that capacity. When Ada Deer arrived for her July 15 confirmation hearings, the Senate Committee on Indian Affairs gave her the unusual honor of a standing ovation. She spoke of her background and heritage and her ongoing work on behalf of her tribe and other Americans. "Hope, healing, commitment, and change are in the skies all around us," she told them. Deer was easily confirmed in one day instead of the usual 72 hours, then sworn in by Secretary of the Interior Bruce Babbitt on July 16.

Ada Deer says that her mother inspired her with this message: "You are put on this Earth to help others." As a college student, Deer had visited Washington to speak out about things that concerned her. Now the "dreamer with power" had come to the nation's capital, bringing energy, enthusiasm, and a wealth of practical experience. Fortified with many years of speaking out and working hard, Ada Deer was ready to go on doing what she calls "enhancing the human condition" in the nation's capital.

WILMA MANKILLER

◆ ◆ ◆

First Woman Chief of the Cherokee

Wilma Mankiller was born more than a century after the Trail of Tears. But the memories of that tragic journey were passed down to her, for Mankiller's ancestors were among the Cherokee who survived the trip to Oklahoma. Her tribe had experienced many ups and downs after arriving in Indian Territory. In 1907 the tribe's lands were made part of the state of Oklahoma. The Cherokee Nation as a legal entity was dissolved, and tribal lands were allocated to individual Cherokees. The U.S. president even appointed their tribal chiefs until 1971, when federal self-determination legislation formally reestablished the Cherokee Nation. Because the reservation lands had been divided, with some being sold, the Cherokee were given an area in Oklahoma containing some 55,000 acres.

Like her ancestors, Wilma Mankiller is a triumphant survivor. She has overcome poverty and severe health problems to become a respected leader among her tribe and on the national scene. Mankiller has said that, in a sense, overcoming adversity has been a positive experience: "I came out of it with a much greater understanding of what I wanted to do with my life. Having survived all that, I knew I could survive anything. Any other problems are minor."

◆ ◆ ◆

Wilma Mankiller was born in Tahlequah, Oklahoma, the Cherokee capital, on November 18, 1945. In all, the family had 11 children. Wilma's mother Irene was of Dutch-Irish descent, while her father was Cherokee. Charlie Mankiller was a leader among his people and an Indian rights activist. Their family name came from an 18th-century warrior named Mankiller of Tellico.

Until Wilma was 12, the family lived on Mankiller Flats, the land her grandfather had received from the U.S. government. There, in a rural, wooded area of Adair County, Oklahoma, the Mankillers raised peanuts and strawberries. The children helped with the crops and with growing their own food, as well as bringing water to the house from a quarter mile away.

During these years, the family farm suffered from the severe droughts in the region. By 1957, it seemed clear that they could not make a living at Mankiller Flats. The family moved to Hudson Point, a poor, high-crime neighborhood in downtown San Francisco. Along with other rural Indians, Charlie Mankiller took part in a federal program that found jobs for them in cities throughout America. He worked in a warehouse and on the docks, then became a union organizer.

As hard as her father worked, his wages barely supported the family, so Wilma learned first-hand about urban poverty, as she had come to know rural poverty in Oklahoma. There was only one other Cherokee family in their area, so the Mankillers were cut off from their customary social ties and group traditions. Things such as telephones and indoor plumbing were new and strange to the children. The first time Wilma heard a siren at night, she was terrified. She has since said that urban poverty is much worse than rural poverty, because "the violence was everywhere."

Despite these disadvantages, Wilma worked hard and was highly motivated to gain an education. She attended San Francisco State University, majoring in sociology and community development. While there, Wilma met and married a wealthy professor from Ecuador. They had two daughters, Felicia (now Felicia Swake), born in 1964, and Gina (now Gina Olaya), born in 1966. For the first time, Wilma had no money problems to worry her, and she concentrated on being a homemaker and a good mother.

During those years, an organization called the American Indian Movement (AIM) was growing, along with the black civil rights movement and other minority rights movements of the 1960s. In 1969 Mankiller witnessed a historic event when AIM members took control of the former, remote prison island of Alcatraz in San Francisco Bay. Raising money for their cause and listening to speeches by AIM members led to what Mankiller later called her "political awakening." She knew first-hand about the problems and living conditions of poor Indians in America. Now her interest in helping her people was strongly aroused.

When her marriage ended in 1976, Mankiller took her daughters back to Oklahoma. She built a small house on her grandfather's land, finished her bachelor's degree, and took a job with the Cherokee Nation to develop economic projects for the tribe. Like her father, who had died in 1971, Mankiller found she had a knack for organizing people and getting things done. For three years, she devised plans and wrote applications for economic grants that would bring government funding for the various projects. As she found ways to bring important services to rural people, she became widely known as a hard worker and an activist.

Eager for more education, Mankiller enrolled in graduate school at the University of Arkansas. On November 9, 1979, she was driving home from classes on State Highway 100 when a tragic accident occurred. Her best friend, who was traveling in the opposite direction away from Tahlequah, passed a line of cars and hit Mankiller's station wagon head on. Severely injured herself, Mankiller also had to deal with the grief of her friend's death.

For months, Mankiller endured numerous operations to repair her face and legs, which had been shattered in the collision. Her right leg was hurt so badly that doctors thought it should be amputated. Thanks to a gifted surgeon and 17 operations, she was able to keep her leg and begin the painful process of learning to move and walk again. Even after this, her leg still hurt and she had a limp.

As if these ordeals were not enough, Mankiller found that she was slowly losing control of muscles all over her body. She described this weakness to doctors, saying she could not keep her balance and that she often dropped things. While watching a television program about muscular dystrophy, Mankiller heard about a disease called myasthenia gravis, which causes nerves to malfunction. She became convinced that that was her problem, and doctors verified the diagnosis.

This period of poor health proved to be an incredibly difficult time, during which Mankiller said she spent a lot of time thinking about her spiritual heritage—what the Cherokee call "being of a good mind." This philosophy stresses thinking positively, accepting all humans as family, and moving forward from the past to a better future. Mankiller has since said that this time of reflection helped her become a better leader.

She needed a great deal of spiritual strength, for in 1980, Mankiller was hospitalized again, this time for surgery on her thymus gland and to repair muscle and nerve damage in her chest caused by the progression of her disease. She recalls, "My head wouldn't hold up. My eyes didn't work right." For six years after the surgery, she had to take steroid medications that caused upsetting side effects. Finally, the myasthenia gravis seemed to be gone.

Despite all her problems, Mankiller worked actively during the early 1980s. She developed a program that helped a group of Cherokee in Bell, Oklahoma build a 26-mile water line for their community. With materials from the federal government, the Cherokee used their technical expertise and called upon Indians and non-Indians in Bell to provide the needed labor. Afterward, the people in Bell joined forces to complete more public projects, including a senior citizens' center and a fire department. Besides this, as founder and first director of the Cherokee Nation's Community Development Department, she planned other self-help programs and helped to improve housing and education.

Ross Swimmer, principal chief of the Cherokee, decided Mankiller would make a fine deputy, and he asked her to run for election with him in 1983. Swimmer was a highly regarded leader who had implemented the new Cherokee constitution. When they won, Mankiller became the first woman deputy chief in Cherokee history.

Chief Wilma Mankiller in her office at Tahlequah, Oklahoma. In 1985, Mankiller became the first woman to serve as principal chief of the Cherokee Nation. (Cherokee Nations Communications)

In 1985 Swimmer took a new job in Washington, D.C., at the Bureau of Indian Affairs. Now Mankiller was eligible to assume the role of principal chief, but she recalls being reluctant to take over this role. She went swimming, an exercise she does regularly for fitness and to improve the strength in her leg. As she swam, she thought about the job and decided she would do it, thus becoming the first woman to hold the office of principal chief.

The next year Mankiller remarried. Her husband, Charlie Soap, is a bilingual Cherokee whom she had known for years. She was also elected to Oklahoma Women's Hall of Fame and named American Indian Woman of the Year by the Oklahoma Federation of Women. Her contributions were noted in other parts of the country when she received a citation for Outstanding Contributions to American Leadership and Native American Culture from the Harvard Foundation at Harvard University and an honorary doctorate from the University of New England.

This attention gave Mankiller a forum in which to discuss the contributions and concerns of Native Americans, something very important to her. She once said, "Sometimes I think the United States has been slow to recognize the contributions of Native Americans, because it simply does not want to deal with the truth about the history of America. No one wants to hear about the Sand Creek Massacre, the Trail of Tears, the incredible brutality toward California Indians or the Wounded Knee Massacre. They don't want to hear about the democracies that existed on this continent when there were still aristocracies in Europe. . . . They want us to be invisible so they can hang onto their myths about the brave frontier families."

Mankiller was reelected as principal chief in 1987, after first proving to people she could do the job well. It was a historic event, the first time a woman had been elected on her own as principal chief of any tribe. Wilma Mankiller received 56 percent of the vote. She gave credit to her husband for his help in her election. Charlie Soap had campaigned on her behalf to convince conservative male voters that a woman chief was not only acceptable but part of Cherokee heritage. Sexism, Soap pointed out, had not been part of Cherokee culture but had been introduced to them by European settlers. Among the other honors Mankiller received in 1987 was the Woman of the Year award given by *Ms.* magazine. The next year, she was selected to receive the San Francisco State University Alumna of the Year Award and was named one of the 100 most important women in America by the *Ladies' Home Journal*. More honors came her way in 1989 and 1990—the John W. Gardner Leadership Award from the U.S. Public Health Service; International Women of Distinction, Alpha Delta Kappa; the Indian Health Service Award from the U.S. Public Health Service for her work in developing rural health clinics; and an honorary doctorate in humane letters from Yale University.

In 1990 Mankiller faced another devastating health problem— kidney disease that resulted in the loss of both her kidneys. That June, she underwent a transplant operation, receiving an organ donated by her oldest brother, Donald Mankiller.

Mankiller recovered and resumed her energetic schedule. In a June 1991 election, she was reelected principal chief with 82 percent of the vote. It was a huge margin, one that Mankiller said demonstrated the people's faith in her ability, regardless of her gender. Mankiller kept up a hectic schedule of meetings, organizing projects, and public appearances, also spending time with tribe members who came to her with problems. In 1992, she was inducted into the International Women's Forum Hall of Fame and received the National Racial Justice Award.

Mankiller was reelected to her third term in 1993 and now presides over 105,000 people, managing a budget in excess of $66 million a year. She fights for Indian rights and traditions and often goes to Washington to testify before committees dealing with Indian issues. Employment, education, and health care have always been among her special concerns, along with educating other Americans about Native American ways. Among the Cherokee, the unemployment rate is 15% (twice the national average but better than that of many other Indian tribes). The tribe also has a problem with substandard housing and a low per capita income— $4,300 in 1988, compared to the state average of $6,500. Mankiller is also eager to reduce the high dropout rate among Cherokee students. One of her big successes was increasing the number of reservation jobs by building Cherokee Nation Industries, which runs many businesses. This organization went from losing $1.9 million in 1978 to making about $20 million 10 years later. Mankiller also initiated a Department of Commerce for the Cherokee that oversees the tribe's motel, restaurant, gift shops, and Cherokee Garden businesses. She was pleased at being able to help bring a $9 million vocational training center to her tribe.

Wilma Mankiller meets with a group of Cherokee children. Health, education, and employment have been among her foremost concerns since she began working in tribal politics. (Cherokee Nations Communications)

She also finds moments for pursuing personal interests—her family (which now includes four grandchildren: Aaron Swake, born in 1984; Jaron Swake, born in 1990; Breanna Swake, born in 1991; and Kelly Olaya, born in 1988), reading, cooking, and gardening. One of her money-raising activities has involved writing a cookbook. Her husband Charlie Soap works in community development and has served as head of the Christian Children's Fund for northeastern Oklahoma. They live in Stillwell, in Adair County, where Mankiller lived as a child.

Mankiller is known as a strong and visionary leader who has improved the tribe's economic condition and helped to preserve its unity and culture. She usually rises between 6 A.M. and 8 A.M. and begins taking the first of many phone calls. Her constituents say she is very approachable. "People should feel free to call or drop by. It's better to have people talking to you than to feel isolated," Mankiller has said.

Self-help is her hallmark, and she often says, "Although we've been affected by a lot of historical factors, nobody's going to pull us out but ourselves." She also points out, "We need to trust our own thinking and not think that some expert somewhere has better ideas about how we should live and what our future communities should look like." Her friend, Navajo president Petersen Zah, says of her, "She is a visionary who is very aggressive about achieving the goals she has in mind for her people. She truly cares about others."

Since Mankiller became the first, other women have followed as Indian tribal leaders. Now about 8 percent of all tribal chiefs are women—among them Mildred Cleghorn of the Chiricahua Apache; Diane Bailey of the Katzee; and Violet Pachano of the Chisasibi Cree. Regardless of whether they are men or women, other Native American leaders have praised Mankiller's positive, practical approach and successful efforts. In the future, says Mankiller, "I'd like to see whole, healthy communities again, communities in which tribe members would have access to adequate health care, higher education if they want it, a decent place to live, a decent place to work, and a strong commitment to tribal language and culture."

On April 4, 1994, Mankiller announced that she would not seek re-election in 1995. She said, "Almost all of my life I've been blessed with the ability to know when it's time to make a change. . . . it's time for another change for myself and the Cherokee Nation." Mankiller assured supporters that she would stay active in Indian and tribal affairs. Health care and children remained two of her foremost concerns. Among her many accomplishments as chief were three new health centers and nine additional children's programs.

Much of her success, she believes, comes from being a "team player," who works with others to develop projects, following the Cherokee tradition of a "good mind" or positive attitude. She says, "As individual characters or as a tribe as a whole, we have faced adversity in a positive way. You take what's done and turn it to a better path."

SELECTED ANNOTATED BIBLIOGRAPHY

◆ ◆ ◆

General References

Brown, Dee. *Bury My Heart at Wounded Knee: An Indian History of the American West*. New York: Henry Holt, 1971. A realistic look at the treatment of Plains Indians and other western Indian tribes and the many broken treaties as the U.S. government took their ancestral lands; debunks popular myths about the roles of whites and Indians in the "Old West."

Debo, Angie. *A History of the Indians of the United States*. Norman: University of Oklahoma Press, 1970. An overview of important events in the history of various tribes, concentrating on the years after white contact.

Deloria, Vine. *American Indian Policy in the Twentieth Century*. Norman: University of Oklahoma Press, 1985. A summary of changing government policies toward Native Americans during this century by a well-known Sioux author.

Forbes, Jack D., ed. *The Indian in America's Past*. Englewood Cliffs, NJ: Prentice Hall, 1964. Selected articles that show the diverse contributions Native Americans have made to American life.

Gallant, Roy. *Ancient Indians: The First Americans*. Hillside, NJ: Enslow, 1989. For young adults. A look at ancient Indian groups and their various cultures, and how they have been influenced by geography and the regional food supply.

Jones, Jane Clark. *The American Indian in America*. Minneapolis, MN: Lerner, 1991–92. For young people; a two-volume history of Indian life in North America.

Josephy, Alvin M., Jr. *Red Power: The American Indians' Fight for Freedom*. New York: American Heritage Press, 1971. A well-known writer on Native American history focuses on the Indian rights movement in the 1960s and 1970s—the American Indian Movement along with other groups and their leaders.

Kelly, Lawrence C. *Federal Indian Policy*. New York: Chelsea House, 1989. Written for young adults; follows changing U.S. government policies toward Native Americans through the turbulent Indian removals of the 1800s to the present; examines the effects of treaties and reservations, as well as assimilation, termination, and other policies.

Nabokov, Peter, ed. *Native American Testimony: A Chronicle of Indian-White Relations From Prophecy to the Present, 1492–1992*. New York: Viking Penguin, 1992. Documentary history by Native Americans covering a wide variety of tribes and historic events.

Washburn, Wilcomb E., ed. *The American Indian and the U.S.: A Documentary History*. Westport, CT: Greenwood Press, 1973. Four volumes of Native American history as seen by the participants.

Deganawidah and Hayenwatha

Arden, Harvey. "The Fire That Never Dies." *National Geographic* (September 1987): pp. 374–403. A look at the Iroquois people today, with some history about the formation of the confederacy and the tradition of the council fire; lavishly illustrated.

Colden, Cadwallader. *The History of the Five Indian Nations of Canada*. 1727. Reprint. NY: AMS Press, 1973. The author used accounts of meetings between Iroquois leaders and British colonial leaders in writing this history of the Iroquois.

Cornplanter, Jesse J. *Legends of the Longhouse*. Port Washington, NY: Ira J. Friedman, 1963. A Native American author recounts Iroquois stories, myths, and legends.

Dockstader, Frederick J. *Great Native American Indians: Profiles in Life and Leadership*. New York: Van Nostrand, 1977. Brief profiles of major and some lesser-known Indian leaders, with illustrations for most profiles. Includes Deganawidah and Hayenwatha.

Fagan, Brian M. *Clash of Cultures*. New York: W. H. Freeman, 1984. A discussion of the problems faced by Native Americans in dealing with the vastly different values and attitudes of white Europeans who settled in the Americas.

Farb, Peter. *Man's Rise to Civilization*. New York: Dutton, 1978. Discusses early history of Iroquois, especially their tribal organization and spiritual beliefs; describes the role of Deganawidah in the formation of the League.

Graymont, Barbara. *The Iroquois*. New York: Chelsea House, 1988. Written for young adults; a discussion of Iroquois life from the time of Hayenwatha to the present day by an expert on Iroquois history.

Henry, Thomas R. *Wilderness Messiah: The Story of Hiawatha and the Iroquois*. New York: William Sloane Associates, 1955. A colorful account of the great Iroquois chief who played a major role in the building of the confederacy.

Jennings, Francis, ed. *The History and Culture of Iroquois Diplomacy: An Interdisciplinary Guide to the Treaties of the Six Nations and Their League*. Syracuse, NY: Syracuse University Press, 1985. A discussion of the Iroquois system of government and their treaties.

Johansen, Bruce E. *Forgotten Founders: Benjamin Franklin, the Iroquois, and the Rationale for the American Revolution*. Boston: Harvard Common Press, 1982. A discussion of Iroquois institutions and government, and their influence on Franklin and other political thinkers.

———. *Forgotten Founders: How the American Indian Helped Shape Democracy*. Boston: Harvard Common Press, 1987. A new edition of the earlier book, emphasizing the contributions of Native American political ideas to the new ideas about democracy embraced by whites who came from monarch-ruled Europe to settle North America.

Josephy, Alvin M., Jr. *The Patriot Chiefs*. New York: Viking, 1961. Chapter One, "The Real Hiawatha," describes Iroquois history and the tribe's first encounters with French explorers.

Morgan, Lewis Henry. *League of the Ho-De-No-Sau-Nee, or Iroquois*. New York: Corinth Books, 1962. Originally published in 1851; an anthropologist's history of the Iroquois, describing their form of government and their community life.

Richter, Daniel, and Merrell, James, eds. *Beyond the Covenant Chain: The Iroquois and Their Neighbors in Indian North America: 1600–1800*.

Syracuse, NY: Syracuse University Press, 1987. Iroquois history during the development and early years of the confederacy.

Weatherford, Jack. *Indian Givers: How the Indians of the Americas Transformed the World*. New York: Crown, 1988. Discusses the various contributions made by Native Americans, including ideas and political influence as well as food, clothing, housing, and recreation.

Seathl

Buerge, David. "The Man We Call Seattle." *The* [Seattle] *Weekly* (June 29–July 5, 1983): pp. 24–37. An in-depth look at the life and times of Seathl, describing both his personal life and his years as tribal leader.

Egan, Timothy. "Chief's 1854 Lament Linked to Ecological Script of 1971." *New York Times* (April 21, 1992): pp. A-1, A-17. A discussion about the current controversy over the actual speeches of Chief Seathl versus quotations written by others that have been falsely attributed to him.

"The Famous Oration of Chief Seattle." Seattle, WA: Washington State Museum of History and Industry (n.d.). Contains the letter from Dr. Henry A. Smith, first published in the *Seattle Sunday Star* on October 29, 1887, in which he translates the chief's 1854 speech into English.

Gerber, Peter R., trans. by Barbara R. Fritzmeier. *Indians of the Northwest Coast*. New York: Facts On File, 1989. Vivid description of the history and life-styles of Pacific coastal Indians, including Alaska natives; lavishly illustrated with paintings, photographs, and examples of Native American arts and crafts; extensive bibliography.

Stevens, Hazard. *Life of Isaac Ingalls Stevens*. New York: Houghton, 1904. The life and career of the white official who was sent as governor of the Northwest Territory in 1855 to oversee the growing white settlements and to negotiate with regional Indians to move them onto reservations.

John Ross

Carter, Samuel III. *Cherokee Sunset: A Nation Betrayed*. Garden City, NY: Doubleday, 1976. A history of the Cherokee, emphasizing the period from the mid-1700s through the years following their removal to Indian Territory. Many quotes and photographs; extensive source notes and bibliography.

Eaton, Rachel Caroline. *John Ross and the Cherokee Indians* (a dissertation presented in 1919). Chicago, IL: University of Chicago Press, 1921. A full-length biography of the leader, describing his life and times and the history of the Cherokee; includes quotations and sources.

Edmunds, R. David, ed. *American Indian Leaders: Studies in Diversity*. Lincoln, NE: University of Nebraska Press, 1980. Detailed profile of John Ross, his ancestry, life, and work, with source notes.

Jahoda, Gloria. *The Trail of Tears: The Story of the American Indian Removals, 1813–1855*. New York: Holt, Rinehart, and Winston, 1975. The author interviewed members of the Cherokee and other tribes and used original documents for the many quotations. Source notes and chapter-by-chapter bibliography.

Moulton, Gary E. *John Ross, Cherokee Chief*. Athens: University of Georgia Press, 1978. Comprehensive biography, with material from official documents and letters.

Wilkins, Thurman. *Cherokee Tragedy*. New York: Macmillan, 1970. The story of the Cherokee Removal, including previous history in the Southeast; profiles of Ross, Watie, and the Ridges.

Washakie

Brown, James S. *Life of a Pioneer*. Salt Lake City: George Q. Cannon & Sons, 1900. Description of life in the Green River settlement where Mormons lived with Shoshone as farmers and missionaries.

Furness, Norman F. *The Mormon Conflict*. New Haven, CT: Yale University Press, 1966. Discusses the relationship between the Shoshone and Mormon settlers of Utah during the mid-1800s.

Lewis, Meriwether. *The Journals of Lewis and Clark*. Edited by Bernard de Voto. Boston: Houghton Mifflin, 1953. Account of the Lewis and Clark expedition from the detailed diary of Meriwether Lewis; describes their meetings with the Shoshone and the role of Sacajawea, the Shoshone guide and interpreter for the group.

Trenholm, Virginia C., and Carley, Maurine. *The Shoshonis: Sentinels of the Rockies*. Norman: University of Oklahoma Press, 1964. Comprehensive history of the tribe and its notable members; includes quotations from Washakie and terms of the various treaties made between his group and government officials.

Wright, Peter M. "Washakie." In Edmunds, R. David, *American Indian Leaders: Studies in Diversity*. Lincoln: University of Nebraska Press, 1980. Detailed portrait of Washakie's life and historical events that affected him and his tribe.

Black Kettle

Berthrong, Donald J. *The Southern Cheyennes*. Norman: University of Oklahoma Press, 1963. A history of the Southern Cheyenne with an account of the 1864 war.

Debo, Angie. *A History of the Indians of the United States*. Norman: University of Oklahoma Press, 1970. Comprehensive Native American history; discusses the massacres at Sand Creek and Washita.

Dockstader, Frederick J. *Great Native American Indians: Profiles in Life and Leadership*. New York: Van Nostrand, 1977. Brief profiles of major and lesser-known leaders; illustrations for most profiles.

Grinnell, George Bird. *The Cheyenne Indians*. Norman: Oklahoma University Press, 1915. Detailed history of the Cheyenne before and after they divided into Northern and Southern groups.

———. *The Fighting Cheyennes*. New York: Scribner's, 1961. Focuses on the war chiefs and on battles against both enemy tribes and white settlers and troops.

————. *Pawnee, Blackfoot, and Cheyenne*. New York: Scribner's, 1961. Discusses the daily lives of these three Plains tribes, as well as their history and religions.

Hoig, Stanley. *The Cheyenne*. New York: Chelsea House, 1989. For young people. A detailed history of the Cheyenne from ancient times to the present day—their geography, daily life, spiritual traditions, important leaders, and their lives today.

————. *The Peace Chiefs of the Cheyennes*. Norman: University of Oklahoma Press, 1980. A detailed profile of Black Kettle and other leaders.

Hyde, George E. *The Life of George Bent*. Edited by Savoie Lottinville. Norman: University of Oklahoma Press, 1968. Taken from Bent's letters; includes description of the Sand Creek Massacre as told by George Bent, the son of trading post owner William Bent and his Cheyenne wife.

Lewis, Meriwether. *The Journals of Lewis and Clark*. Edited by Bernard de Voto. Boston: Houghton Mifflin, 1953. An account of the Lewis and Clark expedition from the detailed diary of Meriwether Lewis; describes details of everyday life and Indian culture, food, and dress.

Llewellyn, Karl N., and Hoebel, E. Adamson. *The Cheyenne Way*. Norman: University of Oklahoma Press, 1932. History, myths, and life-style of the Cheyenne people.

Ouray

Debo, Angie. *A History of the Indians of the United States*. Norman: University of Oklahoma Press, 1970. An overview of important events in the history of various tribes; concentrates on the years after white contact.

Dockstader, Frederick J. *Great Native American Indians: Profiles in Life and Leadership*. New York: Van Nostrand, 1977. Brief profiles of major and lesser known leaders; illustrations for most profiles.

Haines, Frances. *Indians of the Great Basin and Plateau*. New York: Putnam's, 1970. For young readers; describes life-styles and major historical events of these two culture groups from ancient times to the present. A discussion of the Ute and their relocation to a reservation, and of present-day problems, is included in the discussion of Great Basin groups.

Handbook of North American Indians: Vol. 2, Great Basin, 1986. A detailed reference book that covers the history, culture, legends, religious customs, and current activities of tribes in this culture group, including the Ute, Shoshone, and others. Illustrated.

Crowfoot

Ewers, John C. *The Blackfeet: Raiders on the Northwestern Plains*. Norman: University of Oklahoma Press, 1958. A history of the Blackfoot, describing their way of life and conflicts with other Plains tribes.

Grinnell, George Bird. *Pawnee, Blackfoot, and Cheyenne*. New York: Scribner's, 1961. An account of the culture, customs, and beliefs of these three Plains tribes.

Hungry-Wolf, Beverly. *The Ways of My Grandmothers*. New York: William Morrow, 1980. A member of the Blackfoot of Canada describes the history, customs, and life-styles of her tribe, especially of the women. Discusses the importance of handing down traditions.

McLuhan, T. C. *Touch the Earth: A Self-Portrait of Indian Existence*. New York: Promontory Press, 1991. Quotes a variety of Native Americans throughout history on numerous subjects; includes sources and suggestions for further reading.

Monture, Ethel Brant. *Canadian Portraits: Brant, Crowfoot, Oronhyatekha*. Toronto: Clarke, Irwin, and Co., 1960. Biographies of three major chiefs who led Canadian tribes in turbulent times.

Morris, Alexander. *The Treaties of Canada With the Indians of Manitoba and the North-West Territories*. Toronto (n.d.). Includes the provisions of the Treaty of 1877, signed by Crowfoot and the Blood and Piegan chiefs.

Samek, Hana. *The Blackfoot Confederacy: 1800–1920*. Albuquerque: University of New Mexico Press, 1987. Compares the policies of the United States and Canada toward the Blackfoot peoples whose lands were located on both sides of the border between those nations.

Spotted Tail

Dockstader, Frederick J. *Great Native American Indians: Profiles in Life and Leadership*. New York: Van Nostrand, 1977. Brief profiles of major and some lesser-known Indian leaders; illustrations for most profiles.

Eastman, Charles A. (Ohiyesa, Sioux). *Indian Heroes and Great Chieftains*. Boston: Little, Brown, 1918. Account of Spotted Tail's life by a Native American. Some of Eastman's details have been disputed by other authors, among them George Hyde.

Hyde, George. *Spotted Tail's Folk: A History of the Brulé Sioux*. Norman: University of Oklahoma Press, 1976. Detailed, documented account of the Brulé Sioux and their history; covers the life of Spotted Tail and other important leaders, weaving their stories into the text.

McLaughlin, James. *My Friend, The Indian*. Boston: Houghton Mifflin Company, 1910. Reminiscences of a man who served in the Bureau of Indian Affairs as an Indian agent among the Sioux and other tribes. Includes first-person accounts and interviews with elder tribal members who recall their history.

Seymour, Flora Warren. *Women of Trail and Wigwam*. New York: Woman's Press, 1930. Includes a profile of Appearing Day, the Brulé Sioux woman who was Spotted Tail's first wife.

Winema (Tobey Riddle)

Keyworth, C. L. *California Indians*. New York: Facts On File, 1990. For young people. A description of the tribes in this geographical region, their life-styles, spiritual beliefs, history, and lives since white contact.

Meacham, Hon. Alfred Benjamin. *Wi-Ne-Ma (the Woman-Chief) and Her People*. Hartford, CT: American Publishing Company, 1876. Written by a former superintendent of Indian affairs who also served as chairman of the 1873 Modoc Peace Commission and worked with Winema. The author credits Winema with saving his life in this story of the Modoc and their leaders.

Murray, Keith A. *The Modocs and Their War*. Norman: University of Oklahoma Press, 1959. Comprehensive account of the Modoc War and the background of the tribe; written by former ranger-historian at Lava Beds National Monument. Extensive list of sources and recommended readings.

Riddle, Jeff C. *An Indian History of the Modoc War*. Eugene, OR: Urion Press, 1914. The son of Winema and Frank Riddle wrote this book based on his personal recollections and the stories told by his parents and other Modoc he lived among on and off the reservation. Contains brief biographies of Winema, Frank Riddle, and important white officials of the day. Includes copies of letters and other documents that relate to the events.

Seymour, Flora Warren. *Women of Trail and Wigwam*. New York: Woman's Press, 1930. A brief profile of Winema is included in these lively stories of various Native American women.

Annie Dodge Wauneka

Anderson, Owanah. *Ohoyo One Thousand: A Resource Guide of American Indian/Alaska Native Women*. Wichita Falls, TX: Ohoyo Resource Center, 1982. Includes more than 1,000 brief biographies of Native American women.

Chanin, Abe, with Chanin, Mildred. *This Land, These Voices* ("The Daughter of the Lost Navajo Chief"). Flagstaff, AZ: Northland Press, 1977. An interview with Wauneka; she discusses Navajo history, including the Long Walk; her father's life and work; and her own efforts to improve the lives of her people.

Nelson, Mary Carol. *Annie Wauneka*. Minneapolis, MN: Dillon Press, 1972. A biography for young people, ages 9 to 13, that includes information about Wauneka's ancestry, childhood, personal life, and work to help her people.

Waltrip, Lela and Waltrip, Rufus. *Indian Women*. New York: David McKay, 1964. Biographical sketch of Annie Dodge Wauneka explores her work for Navajo health services and other contributions. Twelve other women, dating from 1535 to the 1900s, are also profiled.

Yazzie, Ethelou. *Navajo History*. Rough Rock, AZ: Navajo Curriculum Center, 1971. Includes Navajo legends, as well as events through history.

Ada Deer

"Ada Deer for Congress." *The Capital Times*. (Madison, WI) (August 27, 1992): op. ed. An endorsement of Deer's candidacy; describes her experience and achievements.

"Ada Deer's Activism Sets a New Pace." *The Daily Cardinal* (St. Louis, MO) (October 29, 1992): p. 2. A look at Ada Deer's unorthodox and grass-roots political campaign.

"Citizen Candidate: Deer Should Be Nominated." *Milwaukee Sentinel*. (September 3, 1992): p 12-A. Editorial endorsement of Deer's candidacy for Wisconsin's Second Congressional District.

Deer, Ada with Simon, R.E., Jr. *Speaking Out*. Chicago: Children's Press, 1970. Deer's autobiography, covering her childhood, education, tribal activism, and career up to 1970.

"Deer: 'Me, Nominee.'" *Wisconsin State Journal* (September 9, 1992): pp. A, 1–2. Covers Deer's speech after receiving the Democratic nomination for the Second Congressional District.

Hasson, Judi. "GOP Gang of Outsiders Struggling to Stay Inside." *USA Today* (October 29, 1992): p. 1. Discussion of the campaign between Deer and Scott Klug, her opponent for the congressional seat from Wisconsin's Second District.

Katz, Jane B., ed. *I Am the Fire of Time*. New York: E. P. Dutton, 1977. Profiles of important Native Americans.

Klein, Barry T. *Reference Encyclopedia of the American Indian*. 6th ed. West Nyack, NY: Todd Publications, 1993. Summary of Deer's major achievements, awards, and board memberships.

"The Menominee Are Terminated," from DRUMS testimony, Hearings on Senate Concurrent Resolution 26, Senate Committee on Interior and Insular Affairs, July 21, 1971. The Menominee discuss the problems of being the first tribe to be officially terminated from federal support as a result of the policy introduced during the 1950s.

Spaid, Elizabeth Levitan. "Aiming to Make Electoral History" *The Christian Science Monitor* (October 21, 1992). A look at the Deer campaign, describing how it was run with the help of hundreds of volunteers and on a slim budget that did not include PAC (political action committee) contributions.

Wilma Mankiller

"Cherokee Nation." *Spin Magazine* (November 1991): pp. 89–91. An interview with Jackson Browne and Wilma Mankiller.

"Cherokee Nation Principal Chief Wilma Mankiller." Tahlequah, OK: Cherokee Nation Communications (n.d.). Basic biographical information about Chief Mankiller and the Cherokee organization, published by the Cherokee Nation.

"Chief of the Cherokee." *Southern Living* (November 1986): p. 190. A look at Mankiller's life and her work as chief.

Davis, Rod. "Trail of Triumph." *American Way* (January 13, 1988): pp. 58–61; 100–101. Mankiller's life story, emphasizing the many obstacles she has overcome to become a successful leader.

Devlin, Jeanne M. "Hail to the Chief." *Oklahoma Today* (January–February, 1990): pp. 32–37. Summary of Mankiller's life, career, and work as Cherokee principal chief.

Martin, Patti. "Cherokee Chief Stresses Women's Rights." *Asbury Park Press* (March 6, 1990): pp. B-1–7. Interview and description of Mankiller's life and work, especially her attempts to bring about improved opportunities and her work for Indian rights and women's rights.

Perdue, Theda. *The Cherokee*. New York: Chelsea House, 1989. For young people. Detailed history of the Cherokee and their way of life to the present day.

"Rebirth of a Nation." *Southern Style* (September–October 1987). In this interview, Chief Mankiller shares her experiences as the first Indian woman to be elected to her position as chief; she discusses her plans as she leads the Cherokee at a pivotal time in their history.

Spaid, Elizabeth Levitan. "Rebuilding a Nation." *Los Angeles Times* (October 4, 1992). A discussion of Mankiller's accomplishments in office, with admiring comments from friends and other leaders.

Wallace, Michele. "Women of the Year: Wilma Mankiller" *Ms.* magazine (January 1988): pp. 68–69. Mankiller speaks about her life and work in an article honoring her and other important American women.

INDEX

Boldface numbers indicate main headings.

Italic numbers indicate illustrations.